DAILY CITIZE
EXTRA.

ASSASSINATION
OF THE
PRESIDENT.

He was Shot at the
THEATRE.

He Died at two minutes
after 7, this morning.

THE NATION IN MOURNING

J. Wilkes BOOTH,
The Actor,
THE ASSASSIN.

ESCAPE OF THE
ASSASIN!

DEATH OF SEC.
SEWARD.

he fired one charge from
which took effect in the
the President's head. T
through and came out at th
Capt Rathburn who was i
Mr. Lincoln attempted to
derer, and on so doing he
in his arm. The assasin t
the box to the stage. B
peared behind the curtai
with a tragic tone and
knife, shouted "*Syc Sem*

So sudden was the aff
moments after the occu
ence supposed that it
play, and were only u
manager announcing fr
President of the Unite
shot. The shock fell
like a thunder bolt, a
immediately raised t
assassin."

The murderous er
power escaped easily:
Theatre, mounted a h
The mass of evide
J. Wilkes Booth c
Whoever it was, th
thinking that the sa
hand attempted the
The person who
a man about thirty
five feet nine inch

✶✶JAMES L.✶✶
SWANSON

CHASING
LINCOLN'S
KILLER

SCHOLASTIC
PRESS
NEW YORK

For my parents,
Lennart & Dianne Swanson

TEXT COPYRIGHT © 2009 BY JAMES L. SWANSON. ALL RIGHTS RESERVED. PUBLISHED BY SCHOLASTIC PRESS, AN IMPRINT OF SCHOLASTIC INC., PUBLISHERS SINCE 1920. SCHOLASTIC, SCHOLASTIC PRESS, AND ASSOCIATED LOGOS ARE TRADEMARKS AND/OR REGISTERED TRADEMARKS OF SCHOLASTIC INC. NO PART OF THIS PUBLICATION MAY BE REPRODUCED, STORED IN A RETRIEVAL SYSTEM, OR TRANSMITTED IN ANY FORM OR BY ANY MEANS, ELECTRONIC, MECHANICAL, PHOTOCOPYING, RECORDING, OR OTHERWISE, WITHOUT WRITTEN PERMISSION OF THE PUBLISHER. FOR INFORMATION REGARDING PERMISSION, WRITE TO SCHOLASTIC INC., ATTENTION: PERMISSIONS DEPARTMENT, 557 BROADWAY, NEW YORK, NY 10012.

ALL INTERIOR AND JACKET ART COURTESY OF THE AUTHOR'S PERSONAL COLLECTION EXCEPT: PP. IV, V, 6 (TOP), 19, 32, 145, 183 (ALL), 184 (TOP), 185 (TOP), AND 188 (BOTTOM RIGHT) COURTESY OF THE LIBRARY OF CONGRESS; P. 94 COURTESY OF DR. SAMUEL A. MUDD HOUSE AND MUSEUM; P. 18 COURTESY OF THE SURRATT SOCIETY; PP. 188 (TOP AND BOTTOM RIGHT) AND 189 COURTESY OF THE SMITHSONIAN INSTITUTION; P. 50 (RIGHT), 169 (TOP) COURTESY OF SEWARD HOUSE. MAP ILLUSTRATION P. 198 BY JIM MCMAHON

LIBRARY OF CONGRESS CATALOGING-IN-PUBLICATION DATA

SWANSON, JAMES L.

CHASING LINCOLN'S KILLER / JAMES L. SWANSON.
P. CM.
ISBN-13: 978-0-439-90354-7
ISBN-10: 0-439-90354-8
1. BOOTH, JOHN WILKES, 1838–1865 — JUVENILE LITERATURE. 2. ASSASSINS — UNITED STATES — BIOGRAPHY — JUVENILE LITERATURE. 3. FUGITIVES FROM JUSTICE — WASHINGTON REGION — BIOGRAPHY — JUVENILE LITERATURE. 4. LINCOLN, ABRAHAM, 1809–1865 — ASSASSINATION — JUVENILE LITERATURE. I. TITLE.
E457.5.B67S93 2009
973.7092 — DC22
[B]
2008017994

48 47 46 45   24 25 26 27

PRINTED IN THE ITALY   183   FIRST EDITION, JANUARY 2009
BOOK DESIGN BY PHIL FALCO

This story is true. All the characters are real and were alive during the great manhunt of April 1865. Their words are authentic. In fact, all text appearing within quotation marks comes from original sources: letters, manuscripts, trial transcripts, newspapers, government reports, pamphlets, books, and other documents. What happened in Washington, D.C., in the spring of 1865, and in the swamps and rivers, forests and fields of Maryland and Virginia during the following twelve days, is far too incredible to have been made up.

The author as a boy

I was born on February 12, Abraham Lincoln's birthday, and my fascination with our sixteenth president began when I was a young boy. On my tenth birthday, my grandmother gave me an unusual present: an engraving of the Deringer pistol John Wilkes Booth used to assassinate Abraham Lincoln, framed by a newspaper article (on page 17) published on the day after the assassination. The newspaper article described some aspects of the assassination, but was cut off before the end of the story. I knew I had to find the rest of the story. This book is my way of doing that.

★★ JAMES L. ★★
SWANSON

★★★★★★★★★★★★★★★★★

FROM
1861
THROUGH 1865,

the United States endured a bloody civil war between Northern and Southern states. The conflict had begun long before over the right to own slaves and states' right to secede, that is, to leave the Union if they disagreed with the government.

In the North, where the economy was based on factories and industry, most citizens considered slavery brutal, inhuman, and immoral. In the South, where the economy was dependent on slave labor, citizens believed they should have the right to own slaves. They also believed that if the national government disagreed with that right, Southern states had the right to secede.

Lincoln, elected president of the United States in 1860 just before the outbreak of the Civil War, held two strong beliefs: that slavery was morally wrong, and that the North and South must remain united as one country.

Southern soldiers, dressed in gray uniforms, were called rebels and Confederates. Northern soldiers, dressed in navy blue uniforms, were referred to as Union soldiers or Yankees.

The war lasted four years and resulted in more than 600,000 casualties, half of them lost to disease. After several bloody battles and costly, prolonged campaigns, Confederate General Robert E. Lee surrendered the Army of Northern Virginia to Union General Ulysses S. Grant in the Virginia town of Appomattox Court House. But other rebel armies continued fighting in the field. Lee's surrender did not mean the end of the war or of danger. Some Confederate sympathizers mourned the outcome of the war — the "lost cause" — would forever change the Southern way of life, including slavery. Many Southerners were unwilling to give up the lost cause, believing they could continue to fight and eventually win, or die trying. It was a dangerous place and time. With Lee's surrender, soldiers shed their uniforms, turned in their weapons, and rode or walked home to resume their lives. Spies and Confederate sympathizers as well as soldiers filled the Union capital, Washington, D.C. People could not tell based on clothing, geography, or appearance which side of the conflict people supported. ★★★★★★★★★★★★★★★★★★★★★★★★★★

PROLOGUE

★★★★★★★★★★★★★★★★★★★★★★★★★★★★

It looked like a bad day for photographers. Terrible
winds and thunderstorms had swept through Washington
early that morning, dissolving the dirt streets into a sticky
muck of soil and garbage. The ugly gray sky of the morning of March 4, 1865, threatened to spoil the great day.
Photographer William M. Smith was to take a historic
photograph of the presidential inauguration in front of the
recently completed Capitol dome. Smith framed the view
from the marble statue of George Washington on the lawn
to the top of the dome, crowned by a statue of *Freedom*.
Abraham Lincoln had ordered work on building the Capitol
dome to continue during the war as a sign that the Union
would go on.

Closer to the Capitol, Alexander Gardner set up his
camera to photograph the inauguration. Gardner captured

1

not only images of the president, vice president, chief justice, and other honored guests occupying the stands, but also the anonymous faces of hundreds of spectators who crowded the east front of the Capitol. In one photograph, on a balcony above the stands, a young man with a black mustache and wearing a top hat gazes down on the president. It is the famous actor John Wilkes Booth.

Abraham Lincoln rose from his chair and walked toward the podium. He was now at the height of his power, with the Civil War nearly won. Clouds threatened another rainstorm. Then the strangest thing happened: The clouds parted and the sun burst out, flooding the spectacle. The president's speech was brief — just 701 words.

"Fondly do we hope — fervently do we pray — that this mighty scourge of war may speedily pass away . . . With malice toward none; with charity for all; with firmness in the right, as God gives us to see the right, let us strive on to finish the work we are in; to bind up the nation's wounds; to care for him who shall have borne the battle, and for his widow, and his orphan — to do all which may achieve and cherish a just and lasting peace, among ourselves, and with all nations."

On April 3, 1865, Richmond, Virginia, capital city of the Confederate States of America, fell to Union forces.

Perhaps the finest portrait of John Wilkes Booth ever made, this magnificent large-format photograph remains vivid evidence of Booth's appeal.

PRESIDENT LINCOLN.

Photographed on the Balcony at the White House,
March 6, 1865, by

WARREN,   WALTHAM.

The last photograph of Abraham Lincoln, taken by Samuel F. Warren on the White House balcony on March 6, 1865

Now it was only a matter of time before the war would finally be over. In the Union capital, emotions were high. The rebellion was almost over, and the victorious North held a celebration. Children ran through the streets waving little paper flags that read WE CELEBRATE THE FALL OF RICHMOND. Across the country, people built bonfires, organized parades, fired guns, shot cannons, and sang patriotic songs.

Four days later, John Wilkes Booth was drinking with a friend at a saloon on Houston Street in New York City. Booth struck the bar table with his fist and regretted a lost opportunity. "What an excellent chance I had, if I wished, to kill the president on Inauguration Day! I was on the stand, as close to him nearly as I am to you."

Crushed by the fall of Richmond, the former rebel capital, John Wilkes Booth left New York City on April 8 and returned to Washington. The news there was terrible for him. On April 9, Confederate General Robert E. Lee and the Army of Northern Virginia surrendered to Union General Grant at Appomattox. Booth wandered the streets in despair.

On April 10, Abraham Lincoln appeared at a second-floor window of the Executive Mansion, as the White House was known then, to greet a crowd of citizens celebrating General Lee's surrender. Lincoln did not have a prepared speech. He used humor to entertain the audience.

Secretary of War Edwin M. Stanton, who organized the manhunt for John Wilkes Booth.

The North rejoiced when the capital of the Confederacy, Richmond, fell on April 3, 1865. This rare broadside celebrated the news but became obsolete less than two weeks later when Lincoln was assassinated.

"I see that you have a band of music with you. . . . I have always thought 'Dixie' one of the best tunes I have ever heard. Our adversaries . . . attempted to appropriate it, but I insisted yesterday we fairly captured it. . . . I now request the band to favor me with its performance."

On the night of April 11, a torchlight parade of a few thousand people, with bands and banners, assembled on the semicircular driveway in front of the Executive Mansion. This time, Lincoln delivered a long speech, without gloating over the Union victory. He intended to prepare the people for the long task of rebuilding the South. When someone in the crowd shouted that he couldn't see the president, Lincoln's son Tad volunteered to illuminate his father. When Lincoln dropped each page of his speech to the floor, it was Tad who scooped them up.

Lincoln continued: "We meet this evening, not in sorrow, but in gladness of heart." He described recent events and gave credit to Union General Grant and his officers for the successful end to the war. He also discussed his desire that black people, especially those who had served in the Union army, be granted the right to vote.

As Lincoln spoke, one observer, Mrs. Lincoln's dressmaker, Elizabeth Keckley, a free black woman, standing a few steps from the president, remarked that the lamplight made him "stand out boldly in the darkness." The perfect target. "What an easy matter would it be to kill the president as he stands there! He could be shot down from the crowd," she whispered, "and no one would be able to tell who fired the shot."

In that crowd standing below Lincoln was John Wilkes Booth. He turned to his companion, David Herold, and objected to the idea that blacks and former slaves would become voting citizens. In the darkness, Booth threatened to kill Lincoln: "Now, by God, I'll put him through."

And as Booth left the White House grounds, he spoke to companion and co-conspirator Lewis Powell: "That is the last speech he will ever give."

On the evening of April 13, Washington celebrated the end of the war with a grand illumination of the city. Public buildings and private homes glowed from candles, torches, gaslights, and fireworks. It was the most beautiful night in the history of the capital.

John Wilkes Booth saw all of this — the grand illumination, the crowds delirious with joy, the insults to the fallen Confederacy and her leaders. He returned to his room at the National Hotel after midnight. He could not sleep.

CHAPTER I

John Wilkes Booth awoke depressed. It was Good Friday morning, April 14, 1865. The Confederacy was dead. His cause was lost and his dreams of glory over. He did not know that this day, after enduring more than a week of bad news, he would enjoy a stunning reversal of fortune. No, all he knew this morning when he crawled out of bed was that he could not stand another day of Union victory celebrations.

Booth assumed that the day would unfold as the latest in a blur of days that had begun on April 3 when the Confederate capital, Richmond, fell to the Union. The very next day, the tyrant Abraham Lincoln had visited his captive prize and had the nerve to sit behind the desk occupied by the first and last president of the Confederate States of America, Jefferson Davis. Then, on April 9, at Appomattox Court House, Virginia, General Robert E. Lee and his beloved Army of Northern Virginia surrendered. Two days later, Lincoln had made a speech proposing to give blacks the right to vote, and last night, April 13, all of Washington had celebrated with a grand illumination of the city. These days had been the worst of Booth's young life.

Twenty-six years old, impossibly vain, an extremely talented actor, and a star member of a celebrated theatrical family, John Wilkes Booth was willing to throw away fame, wealth, and a promising future for the cause of the Confederacy. He was the son of the legendary actor Junius Brutus Booth and brother to Edwin Booth, one of the finest actors of his generation. Handsome and appealing, he was instantly recognizable to thousands of fans in both the North and South. His physical beauty astonished all who saw him. A fellow actor described his eyes as being "like living jewels." Booth's passions included fine clothing, Southern honor, good manners, beautiful women, and the romance of lost causes.

On April 14, Booth's day began in the dining room of the National Hotel, where he ate breakfast. Around noon, he walked over to nearby Ford's Theatre, a block from Pennsylvania Avenue, to pick up his mail: Ford's customarily accepted personal mail as a courtesy to actors. There was a letter for Booth.

That same morning a letter arrived at the theater for someone else. There had been no time to mail it, so its sender, First Lady Mary Todd Lincoln, had used the president's messenger to hand-deliver it to the owners of Ford's Theatre. The mere arrival of the White House messenger told them that the president was coming to the theater tonight! Yes, the president and Mrs. Lincoln would attend this evening's performance of the popular if silly comedy *Our American Cousin*. But the big news was that General Ulysses S. Grant was coming with them.

The Lincolns had given the Fords enough advance notice for the proprietors to decorate and join together the two theater boxes — seven and eight — that, by removal of a partition, formed the president's box at the theater.

By the time Booth arrived at the theater, the president's messenger had come and gone. Some time between noon and 12:30 P.M., as he sat on the top step in front of the entrance to Ford's reading his letter, Booth heard the big news: In just eight hours, the man who was the subject of all his hating and plotting would stand on the very stone steps where he now sat. Here. Of all places, Lincoln was coming here.

Booth knew the layout of Ford's intimately: the exact spot on Tenth Street where Lincoln would step out of his carriage, the box inside the theater where the president sat when he came to a performance, the route Lincoln could walk and the staircase he would climb to the box, the dark underground passageway beneath the stage. He knew the narrow hallway behind the stage where a back door opened to the alley and he knew how the president's box hung directly above the stage.

Though Booth had never acted in *Our American Cousin,* he knew it well — its length, its scenes, its players and, most

An authentic Ford's Theatre playbill for the night of April 14, 1865

important, the number of actors onstage at any given moment during the performance. It was perfect. He would not have to hunt Lincoln. The president was coming to him.

He had only eight hours to prepare. If luck was on his side, there was just enough time to carry out his plan. Whoever told Booth about the president's plan to attend the play that night had unknowingly activated in his mind an imaginary clock that began ticking down, minute by minute. He would have a busy afternoon.

Abraham Lincoln ate breakfast with his family and planned his day. The Lincolns' eldest son, Robert, a junior officer of General Grant's staff, was home from the war. Robert had been at the surrender at Appomattox, and his father was eager to hear the details. General Grant joined Lincoln's cabinet meeting later that day where everyone in attendance, including Secretary of War Edwin M. Stanton and Secretary of the Navy Gideon Welles, noticed Lincoln's good mood. Secretary Welles, who kept a diary, wrote that Lincoln "had last night the usual dream which he had preceding nearly every great and important event of the War. . . . [Lincoln] said [the dream] related to . . . the water; that he seemed to be in some . . . indescribable vessel, and that was moving with great [speed] towards an indefinite shore. . . . [H]e had this dream preceding [the great battles of the Civil War]."

Lincoln had always believed in, and sometimes feared, the power of dreams. In 1863, while visiting Philadelphia, he sent an urgent telegram to Mary Todd Lincoln at the White House, warning of danger to their younger son: "Think you better put Tad's pistol away. I had an ugly dream about him."

After the cabinet meeting ended, the president followed his usual routine: receiving visits from friends and job seekers, reading his mail, and catching up on paperwork. He was eager to wind up business by 3:00 P.M. for an appointment he had with his wife, Mary. There was something he wanted to tell her.

At the theater, Henry Clay Ford wrote out the advertisement that appeared that afternoon in the *Evening Star:*

"LIEUT. GENERAL GRANT, PRESIDENT and Mrs. Lincoln have secured the State Box at Ford's Theatre TO NIGHT, to witness Miss Laura Keene's *American Cousin.*"

James Ford walked to the Treasury Department a few blocks away to borrow several flags to decorate the president's box. On his way back, his arms wrapped around a bundle of brightly colored cotton and silk fabric, he bumped into Booth. They spoke briefly. Booth saw the red, white, and blue flags, further confirmation of the president's visit that night.

Dr. Charles A. Leale, a twenty-three-year-old U.S. Army surgeon, was on duty at the Armory Square Hospital in Washington when he heard that President Lincoln and General Grant would be at the performance that night. He decided to attend. Leale wanted, most of all, to catch a glimpse of the famous general who had won the Civil War.

Booth rode over to the Kirkwood House, where he accomplished his strangest errand of the day. The Kirkwood was the residence of the new vice president, Andrew Johnson, who was from Tennessee. The job did not include official quarters, so he lived at a hotel. Johnson's room was unguarded and, if Booth had wanted to, he could have walked upstairs and knocked on the door, or worse. But he did not want to see or harm the vice president. He just wanted to leave him a note. Booth approached the front desk, wrote a brief note, and handed it to the desk clerk, who placed it in Johnson's mail slot. The message read: "Don't wish to disturb you. Are you at home? J. Wilkes Booth."

Next, Booth visited a boardinghouse on H Street, a few blocks from Ford's Theatre, to pay what looked like an innocent social call on the owner. Mary Surratt was a forty-two-year-old Maryland widow and mother of John Harrison Surratt, a Confederate secret agent and friend of Booth's. Over the last several months, Booth had become a frequent caller at Mrs. Surratt's Washington townhouse. Tonight her son, John, was not home — he was out of the city on rebel business. Mary told Booth that she was riding out that afternoon to her country tavern in Surrattsville, Maryland, several miles south of Washington. Booth asked if she would mind delivering a small package wrapped in newspaper to her tavern. Conveniently, Booth had the package with him.

There was one more thing. Booth told Mary that he would be riding out of Washington this evening. Sometime that night, he said, he would stop at her tavern to pick up not only this package, but also the guns, ammunition, and other supplies that her son, John, had already hidden there for him. He asked Mary to tell the tavern keeper, John Lloyd, to get everything ready for the actor's visit this evening. She agreed, and soon she and Lewis Weichmann, one of her boarders, drove down to Surrattsville by carriage.

At some point that afternoon, Booth made the final arrangements. There were two types of preparation: practical and mental. First, the weapons. Booth chose as his primary weapon a .44 caliber, single-shot, muzzle-loading pistol manufactured by Henry Deringer of Philadelphia. It was a small, short-barreled, pocket-size handgun designed for concealment, not combat. Its big .44 caliber ball, weighing in at nearly an ounce, was a solid, deadly round.

Unlike military pistols that could fire up to six rounds before reloading, the Deringer could be fired just once. Reloading was a time-consuming process that called for two hands and more than twenty seconds. Booth knew that his

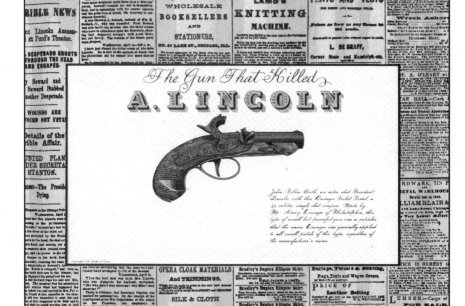

The Gun That Killed A. LINCOLN

John Wilkes Booth, an actor, shot President Lincoln with this Deringer Pocket Pistol, a .44 caliber, single shot weapon. Made by Mr. Henry Deringer of Philadelphia, this type of small but powerful gun was so popular that the name Deringer was generally applied to all small pistols of this type, regardless of the manufacturer's name.

The print of Booth's Deringer pistol

Mary Surratt

Mary Surratt's Washington, D.C., boardinghouse, where the conspirators met, and where Lewis Powell and Mrs. Surratt were arrested

first shot would be his last. If he missed, he wouldn't have time to reload.

Booth left behind no explanation for why he chose the Deringer over a revolver. Pistols misfire occasionally. Either the copper percussion cap might fail to spark, or the black powder in the barrel might fail to ignite because of dampness. Booth was a thrill seeker, so perhaps he wanted to increase his excitement by risking the use of a one-shot pistol. Or did he believe it more heroic, more honorable — even more gentlemanly — to take his prey with a single bullet? Perhaps he preferred a stylish single-shot to blazing away with a six-shooter.

Then, if he missed, or failed to kill the president, he would turn to his backup weapon, a Rio Grande camp knife, a handsome and extremely sharp type of bowie knife.

Before leaving the National Hotel, Booth slid the knife and pistol into his pockets and gathered the rest of his belongings. He planned to travel light that night. In addition to the weapons and his clothing — a black felt slouch hat, black wool coat, black pants, big knee-high black leather riding boots with spurs — he took only a velvet-cased compass, keys, a whistle, a date book, a pencil, some money, a small knife, and a few other small items, including small photographs of five of his favorite girlfriends.

When Mary Surratt and her boarder arrived in Surrattsville, the tavern keeper, John Lloyd, wasn't there. He had left on an errand. Mary waited for him. When Lloyd

A confident Booth, well known for his good looks and fine clothes, in all his splendor, much like he was dressed the night he shot the president

returned, he parked his wagon, climbed down, and began unloading his cargo of fish and oysters.

Mary delivered the message to the tavern keeper John Lloyd: "I want you to have those shooting irons ready; there will be parties here tonight who will call for them."

She handed him Booth's package wrapped in newspaper. The evening callers will want this, too, she explained. And, she added, give them a couple of bottles of whiskey. Her mission accomplished, Mary and Lewis drove back to Washington.

Lloyd followed Mary's instructions. He carried the package upstairs, unwrapped it, and discovered Booth's binoculars. He went to a room where, several weeks ago, John Surratt had shown him how to hide two Spencer carbines between the walls. Lloyd retrieved them and placed them with the binoculars in his bedchamber.

At the Herndon House Hotel, around the corner from Ford's, at around 8:00 P.M., Booth presided over a meeting of some of the conspirators he had recruited over the previous months to strike against President Lincoln. This was not the first time they had assembled to move against the president. They had failed at least once before.

Beginning in 1864, Booth, the young stage star, had pledged his cash, his celebrity, and his connections in hatching a bold plan. He put together a harebrained scheme to kidnap President Lincoln, take him to Richmond, and hold him as a hostage for the Confederacy, in an effort to help win the war for the South.

From the time of Lincoln's election in 1860, there arose several conspiracies to kidnap or murder him. Pro-secession, pro-Southern rebels began mailing death threats to Lincoln before he took office in 1861. Some even sent him jars of poisoned fruit! In one notorious plot of 1861, local rebels schemed to assassinate the president-elect when his railroad train passed through Baltimore on the way to Washington for his first inauguration. But Detective Allan Pinkerton ruined the scheme by persuading Lincoln to pass through the city in disguise, several hours ahead of schedule. Other Lincoln haters threatened to assassinate him on the east front of the Capitol the moment he began to read his inaugural address. During the Civil War, several Southern military officers, as well as a handful of officials in the Confederate Secret Service, considered plots against Lincoln. But big talk was cheap in wartime Washington. As late as January 1865, with the Confederacy in danger of collapse at any moment, not one of the conspiracies resulted in serious action against Abraham Lincoln. At some point, John Wilkes Booth came into contact with sympathetic secret agents in Canada, New York City, Washington, D.C., Maryland, and Virginia.

In late 1864 and early 1865, Booth organized his own little band of conspirators, loyal to him and not the

Confederacy. He recruited a gang who, after he clothed and fed them, paid for their food and drink, and allowed them to enjoy the benefits of his fame and favor, would, he hoped, follow him anywhere — even into a plot to kidnap the president of the United States. Booth and his gang of conspirators — Lewis Powell, David Herold, John Harrison Surratt, and George Atzerodt, as well as Samuel Arnold, Michael O'Laughlen, and others who drifted in and out of his circle — would change cheap talk to big action by kidnapping the president.

On March 17, 1865, Booth and his henchmen planned, like highway robbers, to ambush Lincoln's carriage at gunpoint on a deserted road as he rode home to the Executive Mansion. They would make Lincoln their hostage. Booth's information was incorrect, however, and Lincoln did not arrive as expected. Instead, unbelievably, while Booth and his gang lay in wait on the road on the outskirts of the city, Lincoln was giving a speech at Booth's own hotel, the National!

If only the kidnapping plot had worked! There would have been no torchlight parades, no crowds serenading Lincoln at the Executive Mansion, no little children scampering through the streets with little paper flags with red, white, and blue stars and stripes.

Although his panicked gang scattered after that ridiculous failure, Booth hoped to try again. But events unfolded

BOOTH AND HIS ASSOCIATES.

ATZERODT.

HEROLD.

SPANGLER.

BOOTH.

ARNOLD.

O'LAUGHLIN.

PAYNE.

An 1865 photomontage of John Wilkes Booth and his alleged conspirators

quickly when, eighteen days later, Richmond fell, and then General Lee surrendered.

Lincoln's April 11 speech provoked more violent talk. The president's proposal for a limited black citizenship and voting rights enraged the racist actor. But Booth did nothing. If he was serious about assassinating Lincoln, all he had to do was stroll over to the Executive Mansion, announce that the famous actor John Wilkes Booth wished to see the president, await his turn — which nearly always resulted in a private talk with Lincoln — and then shoot Lincoln at his desk. But that would have been a suicide mission. It would have been difficult to escape the White House.

Incredibly, presidential security was very weak in that era, even during wartime; almost anyone could walk into the Executive Mansion without being searched and request a brief meeting with the president. It was a miracle that no one had yet tried to murder Lincoln in his own office.

Booth would soon turn his anger and violent talk into action.

Now, April 14, 1865, Booth assembled enough men to accomplish another mission. "Booth proposed," aspiring kidnapper George Atzerodt recalled, "that we should kill the president." It would, said Booth, "be the greatest thing in the world." Tonight, at exactly 10:00 P.M., Booth and his henchmen would throw into chaos the Union government by killing its top leaders. That would, they hoped, incite the

Confederacy to continue the war against the Union. George Atzerodt, Lewis Powell, and John Wilkes Booth would strike simultaneously and murder Vice President Johnson, Secretary of State Seward, and President Lincoln.

Atzerodt's assignment was to assassinate the vice president in his room at the Kirkwood House. "You must kill Johnson," Booth told him. Lewis Powell would murder Secretary of State Seward. Seward was certain to be in his bed this night recovering from a serious carriage accident.

David Herold, an experienced outdoorsman, hunter, and tracker, would accompany Lewis Powell, take him to Seward's home, and guide the assassin, unfamiliar with the capital's streets, out of the city where he would meet up with Booth.

Booth claimed the most notorious part in the plot for himself. He would slip into Ford's Theatre and assassinate the president during the play. Powell and Herold, Booth's two most loyal pals, agreed to the plan. Atzerodt had doubts about his assignment. He would not do it, he said. Booth then threatened Atzerodt, implying that he might as well kill Johnson, because if he didn't, Booth would accuse him anyway and get him hanged.

None of Booth's conspirators knew it, but Booth had already implicated all of them! He had entrusted a sealed envelope to a friend and fellow actor, who was to see that the letter it contained was published tomorrow in the newspaper. In the letter, not only did Booth justify the triple assassination, but he signed his henchmen's names to the document as well, sealing their fates.

Atzerodt's reluctance to kill Johnson put the whole plot at risk. Atzerodt knew the details of the assassination plan that was unfolding. If he left that meeting and went to the police, Booth, Powell, and Herold would be finished. Guards would rush to protect those threatened in the plot, and the conspirators would be hunted down. Booth would fail in his mission.

At the Executive Mansion, the Lincolns were behind schedule. It was past 8:00 P.M., and they still had not gotten into their carriage. As the curtain rose at Ford's, the coachman and Lincoln's servant Charles Forbes were on top of the carriage. The Lincolns' private afternoon carriage ride and absence from the mansion had left business unfinished, with several politicians still waiting for an audience with the president.

Earlier that afternoon, Lincoln was happy to be free of the politicians and the burdens of his office. It had been one of the happiest days of his life. At breakfast, son Robert told tales of Lee's surrender. For once, the cabinet meeting was free of crises, battle news, and problems requiring the president's immediate attention. Since Lee's surrender, Lincoln had been more cheerful than at any other time during his presidency. He expected more good news about the surrender of additional Confederate armies.

He wanted to ride alone with Mary on this day. She had been emotionally upset since the death of their eleven-year-old son, Willie, in 1862.

They both took the loss hard. But Abraham Lincoln recovered, and Mary did not. "It was hard to lose the boy," he said. He organized Willie's funeral. Then he threw himself into his work.

Mary was at heart a kind woman, but some critics preferred to criticize her personal quirks — her expensive shopping habits, her jealous temper — rather than praise her good works for soldiers or her absolute loyalty to husband, liberty, and the Union cause.

The demands of the war had been so great that the president spent less and less time with Mary. Lincoln knew that he had to change that now that the war was ending. He wanted to talk to Mary about their future. He walked her to the open carriage, his good mood impossible to miss. Mary Todd Lincoln had noticed his recent optimism and now, during their afternoon carriage ride, she spoke to him about it. "Dear husband, you almost startle me by your great cheerfulness."

Lincoln replied, "We must *both* be more cheerful in the future — between the war and the loss of our darling Willie — we have both been very miserable."

During their leisurely ride, the president told his wife that they must try to be happy again. That he would like to see the Pacific Ocean. That perhaps at the end of his second term in office, they would move to Chicago and he would practice law again. Freed from the troubles of war and death — he would send no more armies of young men to die — Lincoln dreamed of the future. Mary later remembered, "I never saw him so supremely cheerful — his manner was even playful."

That evening, when the Lincolns finally left the White House for Ford's, they picked up their guests. General Grant and his wife had declined Lincoln's invitation and boarded a train headed home instead. Several other couples had also declined the invitation, but Major Rathbone, an army officer, and his fiancée, Clara Harris, accepted.

At 8:00 P.M., the management at Ford's decided not to hold the curtain for the presidential party, and the play began without them. Soon, an employee acting as lookout at Ford's spotted the big black carriage turning down Tenth Street. It slowed to a stop beside the wood platform in front of the theater, constructed especially to assist carriage riders in getting out of their vehicles and avoiding the muddy street. The Lincolns, Henry Rathbone, and Clara Harris exited the carriage. The chief usher escorted them through the lobby, up the winding staircase, and across the first balcony to their theater box. Abraham Lincoln's entry to Ford's Theatre at 8:30 P.M. on April 14, 1865, was majestic and simple. He arrived with no crowd of guards or staff, and no announcement to the audience.

Before the presidential party reached the box, the actors, musicians, and theatergoers became aware of the Lincolns' arrival. The actors onstage stopped performing. To the delight of the crowd, the conductor led his orchestra in "Hail to the Chief," the traditional musical accompaniment to the entrance of the president.

Dr. Charles Leale, seated in the front of the first balcony, about forty feet from the president's box, had arrived in time to witness it all. He watched the audience rise to its feet in enthusiasm and cheer. He looked around, too, and watched as Lincoln "looked upon the people he loved and acknowledged [them] . . . with a solemn bow."

At this supreme moment, the people cheered the man who, after a shaky start in office, learned how to command armies, brought down slavery, and become a most eloquent and moving speaker. And as he promised he would, he had saved the Union. Lincoln stood in the box and bowed to the audience.

The outpouring of emotion from the audience and orchestra, the hissing gaslights, the packed house, the fresh, moist scent of spring in the air, the recent and happy news from the army — all combined to make a magical moment.

Ford's Theatre, site of Abraham Lincoln's assassination

CHAPTER II

Legend has it that John Wilkes Booth was hiding outside in the shadows near the front door of Ford's as the presidential carriage rocked down the dirt street and slowed. Wherever he was, it is almost certain that he somehow watched with his own eyes to be certain that the Lincolns were actually inside the theater. And he probably wondered whether other guests in the box were the type who would pose a threat to his plans. It didn't matter, really; no one was going to stop him from going through with it.

It was now about 9:00 P.M. Time for Booth to go inside the theater for the first time since the Lincolns had arrived. Although the actor had entered the theater after the performance had started, he was still on schedule. The play was like a clock, every word spoken was another tick of the second hand. After hearing some familiar dialogue, Booth would know, to the minute, how much time remained in the performance. He knew that he had at least another hour. He left Ford's.

In a little while, he returned to his alley stable where he had left his rented horse, a bay mare. He led the horse down the alley by the reins to the back door of Ford's Theatre. He asked theater employee Edman Spangler to hold his horse for him. Spangler said he was too busy moving scenery. Another theater employee, named John Peanut for the snack he sold to theater patrons, held the reins of Booth's restless horse while the actor went inside.

Once inside Ford's, Booth wanted to cross behind the stage to the other side of the building where a door led to a narrow passageway that ran to the front of the theater. Booth asked an employee if he could sneak across the stage concealed by scenery. That was impossible, he was told, as a scene that required the full stage was being performed and there was nowhere to hide from the audience by creeping behind the scenery. Instead Booth would have to cross under the stage and emerge on the other side.

Booth lifted a trapdoor and dropped down into darkness. He could hear the wooden planks of the stage creaking overhead, the distant, muffled voices of the actors, and laughter from the audience. He climbed the stairs at the end of the passageway, nudged open the trapdoor, and entered the area that ran lengthwise between Ford's and the saloon next door. He emerged on Tenth Street. Anyone who saw him now would assume he had come down Tenth Street to take in the play. No one in the theater, except a few employees, knew he had a horse waiting out back. There was time for one last drink.

Booth walked into the Star Saloon at around 10:00 P.M. The narrow, dimly lit saloon attracted actors, stagehands, and playgoers from Ford's Theatre next door. Alone, he drank whiskey. Any customers who recognized the handsomest, best-dressed man in Washington kept it to themselves and did not disturb him. Booth slapped a few coins on the bar and left without saying a word. As he exited onto Tenth Street, he noticed the president's carriage, parked and waiting to take Lincoln back home.

In the alley behind Ford's, John Peanut walked Booth's impatient horse back and forth.

It was time. Booth entered the theater lobby, listening to the dialogue onstage. He was still on schedule. He climbed the curving staircase to the balcony, following the same path the Lincolns took to their box. He walked slowly along the wall. One theater patron, still hoping to witness General Grant's arrival, looked up from his first-floor seat and saw a man approaching the box. He recognized Booth.

Booth could see the door of the vestibule that led directly into the president's box. What he saw — what he did not see — surprised him. The door was unguarded. He expected to see an officer, a soldier, or at least a policeman seated there. Instead, seated near, but not blocking the door, was Lincoln's servant, Charles Forbes. Booth showed Forbes something. To this day, no one knows what words they exchanged or what Booth showed him. Was it a letter? Or a calling card? A card with Booth's name on it would open almost any door in Washington. Forbes did not attempt to stop him. Booth turned the doorknob and pushed open the vestibule door. There was no guard! No one stood between him and the president of the United States!

Inside the box, the Lincolns were enjoying themselves, not because of the play, but simply from being together, out of the White House, during their happiest week in Washington. Seated in his rocking chair, perhaps thinking of their carriage ride that afternoon, Lincoln reached out and held Mary's hand. In pretend embarrassment, Mary scolded her husband for his boldness, "What will Miss Harris think of my hanging on to you so?" Lincoln replied to the last words he would ever hear his wife speak, "She won't think anything about it." He smiled at her affection- ately. Booth closed the outer vestibule door behind him so quietly that no one heard anything. Bending down, he felt along the edge of the carpet near the wall for the pine bar — part of a music stand he had hidden there that after- noon. When no one was watching, he had entered Ford's, sneaked into the vestibule and box, and made his pre- parations. He found the bar, grabbed it with both hands, and wedged it quietly, tightly between the wall and the door. Now no one could follow him into the president's box.

The actor's black eyes adjusted to the darkness, while fixing on the only light in the dim room, a faint pinpoint of light coming from the peephole that someone — probably Booth — had bored through a panel of the door into the box. Booth peeked through the dot of light on the door, seeing the interior of the box.

Lincoln sat at the far left of the box, closest to Booth, in his rocking chair. The left side of the president's body turned toward the audience, he faced the stage below. Mary sat to Lincoln's right, seated on a wood chair. On her right was Clara Harris, and next to her, Major Rathbone seated on a sofa. Booth could enter the box and shoot Lincoln without having to get past the major.

Onstage, there were four scenes left before the end of the play. It was around 10:00 P.M. Booth plunged his hands into his pocket and withdrew his weapons. In his right hand was the .44-caliber Deringer pistol, and in his left the sharp Rio Grande camp knife. The actor Harry Hawk entered the stage. It was not yet time — there were too many actors still onstage. Booth listened to the dialogue of the play for his signal. In a few moments, Booth knew, Harry Hawk would be alone onstage and would speak a line guaranteed to produce such energetic laughter that it would drown out the sound of just about anything, including, Booth hoped, the sound of a pistol shot.

Artists demonized John Wilkes Booth with lurid pictures of
him as the devil's disciple. This imaginative image shows
Satan whispering in Booth's ear to murder President Lincoln.

Booth's thumb pulled back the hammer of the Deringer until he heard it cock into firing position. His hand reached for the doorknob. Though he could not see the stage, he could hear the dialogue. Now, Booth knew, only two actors remained onstage. The tension was unbearable. The dialogue spoken onstage no longer sounded like words but like the last ticks of a dying clock winding down. It was 10:13 P.M.

Once Harry Hawk was alone onstage, Booth opened the door and stepped into the president's box. Hawk began reciting the last sentence Lincoln would ever hear, a series of corny insults that delighted the audience.

Lincoln was so near. If Booth wished to, he could reach out and tap him with the muzzle of the pistol. No one in the box had seen or heard him enter. They all continued to watch the action onstage. Booth began the performance he had rehearsed in his mind again and again. He stepped forward toward Lincoln, raised his right arm to shoulder height, and extended the pistol forward. He was so close to the president now that all he had to do was point the Deringer. Booth squeezed the trigger.

The comic line spoken by Harry Hawk, "You sockdologizing old mantrap," was followed by an explosion of laughter from the audience. The black powder charge exploded and spit the bullet toward Lincoln's head. The muzzle flash lighted the box for a moment like a miniature lightning bolt. Had Booth succeeded?

NUMBER 9.]   PRICE, 25 CENTS.   [GET THE BEST.

DAWLEY'S NEW WAR NOVELS

BOOTH

THE ASSASSIN.

Published a few months after the assassination, this work of fiction was filled with exaggerations and lies, but its cover was an accurate depiction of the shooting.

If he had only wounded Lincoln, then the president, even at fifty-six years old, would have been a worthy opponent. The idea of the president fighting back against the young leaping and sword-fighting actor is not as farfetched as it sounds. With his creased and weary-looking face atop a thin, six-foot-four-inch frame, President Lincoln might have looked old and weak. The war had taken its toll, but beneath his baggy coat and trousers, there was a lean and strong body. Too soon doctors would discover and be amazed at the apparent difference in age between his face and his body.

Lincoln had not seen Booth coming. The bullet struck him in the head, on the lower left side, just below the ear. The ball ripped through his chestnut-colored hair, cut the skin, penetrated the skull, and because of the angle of Lincoln's head at the moment of impact, made a diagonal tunnel through Lincoln's brain. The wet brain matter slowed the ball's speed, absorbing enough of its energy to prevent it from exiting the other side of the skull through the president's face. The ball came to rest in Lincoln's brain, behind his right eye.

Lincoln never knew what happened to him. His head dropped forward, his body lost all muscle control and sagged against the rocking chair. The sound of the pistol shot hung in the box for several seconds. It traveled to the stage below and echoed throughout the theater. The pistol shot did startle some people in the audience. Some thought it was part of the play. Some people did not hear it at all.

Major Henry Rathbone, seated in the box just feet away from the president, was an experienced army officer, familiar with the sounds of gunshots. He was the first to realize that something was very wrong. He turned to his left.

The smoke from the gun, now tinted red from the gaslights, partly blocked his vision. Rathbone rose from his seat and stepped in the direction of the president. At that moment, he saw a wild-eyed man, his face ghostly against his black clothes, hair, and mustache. Like a demon, Booth emerged from the cloud of black powder and sprang at him. Rathbone lunged for Booth, grabbing him by the coat. The assassin broke free, shouting "Freedom!" and throwing his right arm up as high as it could reach. Rathbone saw what Booth had clenched in his fist: a large, shiny knife, its blade pointed directly down at him. At the last moment, Rathbone raised his arm to protect himself from what was intended to be a deathblow.

The major grunted in pain. His quick defensive move had saved his life, but the blade sliced through his sleeve and into his upper arm. Blood gushed from the deep wound.

Booth wasted no more time finishing off Rathbone. The clock in his head was still ticking down. If he was going to escape the theater, he had to get out of the box at once. He swung his leg over the side of the railing at the front of the box. By now, some members of the audience had looked up, seeing a man climbing out of the president's box. As Booth positioned for the leap to the stage, Rathbone came at him again, grabbing his coattail. Thrown off-balance, Booth got tangled in the framed portrait of George Washington hanging on the front of the box. One of his riding spurs snagged one of the flags that decorated the box. He managed to free himself and landed, off-balance, but still on his feet. He felt something wrong in his left leg, near the ankle, but there was nothing he could do about it now.

Booth scrambled to center stage, turned to the audience, and stood up straight. Though every second was precious to his escape, he knew that this was his last appearance on the American stage. This would be the performance he would be remembered for. All eyes were on him. He stood still, paused to build suspense, and thrust his bloody dagger victoriously into the air. The gas stage lights shone on the shiny blade now stained with blood. "*Sic semper tyrannis!*" he thundered. It was the state motto of Virginia: "Thus always to tyrants." Then Booth shouted, "The South is avenged!"

Harry Hawk, the only actor onstage when Booth made the leap, did not understand what was happening. Hawk, more than anyone else in the theater, was in the best position to hear the shot and see Booth climb onto the balcony. Hawk had known Booth and was not likely to mistake him. Hawk stood directly in Booth's escape path. When Booth

THE ASSASSINATION OF PRESIDENT LINCOLN

At Ford's Theatre, Washington, on the night of Friday, April 14, 1865.

PUBLISHED BY A. PHARAZYN, 229 SOUTH ST PHILAD'A

Rival publishers competed frantically to produce prints within days of the assassination. This rush to publish sometimes resulted in dramatic but inaccurate depictions. The president's box was higher from the stage, Booth did not sail through the air, and Lincoln did not spring from his chair after being shot.

had nearly reached him, Hawk fled. As Booth moved across the stage heading for the wing, one audience member heard him say to himself, *I have done it!*

Booth fled into the wings, slashing his dagger at anyone who got in his way. The orchestra conductor said he felt Booth's hot breath as the assassin pushed past him and struck at him with the knife. He did not attempt to stop Booth. Nor did anyone in the cast try. Booth had taken all the actors backstage by surprise and rushed past them.

A voice cried out from the president's box, "Stop that man!"

Some in the audience gasped with fright and delight — they still thought it was part of the play.

"Will no one stop that man?" an anguished Major Rathbone again pleaded to the crowd below. Clara Harris shouted out, "He has shot the president!"

CHAPTER III

Less than a mile away, near the White House, all was quiet at the home of Secretary of State William H. Seward. Confined to his bed since a terrible carriage accident the week before, Seward drifted in and out of consciousness. The night of the accident, Seward's face swelled so badly that his children could barely recognize him, and the blood pouring through his nose almost suffocated him. Seward's doctors warned the family to keep him under constant watch.

Four days after the carriage accident, Lincoln walked from the White House to Seward's big brick mansion nearby to check on Seward. The accident worried Lincoln. Carriage accidents were serious in wartime Washington and could prove deadly. The sight of Seward, alive if not well, relieved Lincoln.

During the war, Lincoln and Seward had become good friends and trusted confidants. After talking quietly for an hour, Lincoln left, and never saw Seward again.

Now, on April 14, Fanny Seward watched over her father and listened to the sights and sounds of the celebrations in the streets. A torchlight parade marched to the White House. A band played patriotic songs. Fanny was a tall, slender, brown-haired girl, educated in literature and politics and, at age twenty, her father's favorite. A devoted and talented writer with an eye for detail, her secret diary, which she began at fourteen, detailed her observations and encounters with the political, military, and diplomatic elite.

Outside the mansion, in the shadows, Lewis Powell and David Herold were keeping the Seward house under close watch. The street was quiet. They saw no guards at the front door or anywhere on the street. The newspapers reported Seward's carriage accident and described the serious injuries he had suffered, noting that he was recovering at home, bedridden. That made Seward, of all of Lincoln's cabinet officers, Booth's most appealing target tonight. The other cabinet officers could be anywhere — dinner parties, traveling — and would be difficult to track. Seward, helplessly lying in bed, was sure to be home when the assassins arrived. Booth issued simple instructions to his henchmen: Invade the house, locate the secretary of state's bedroom, and kill the defenseless victim with pistol fire and, if necessary, a knife. This was a difficult mission even for a man like Powell, a battle-hardened and extremely strong ex-Confederate soldier.

Powell had three problems. First, how was he to enter the house? The door surely locked, he would have to ring the bell. If someone answered, could he just shoot or slash his way in? That might attract the attention of pedestrians or awaken the occupants of the house to defend themselves. Deception, not brute force, was the key. They came up with a brilliant plan. Powell would pretend he was a messenger delivering important medicine from Seward's doctor. To make his story more believable, Powell carried a small package wrapped in paper and tied with string.

Powell's second problem was that he would have to track down Secretary Seward himself — not just deliver the package to a servant or nurse. How would he find him in the large three-story mansion?

Powell's third challenge: How many people were in the house? Seward might be attended by nurses, doctors, servants, maids, family members, and guards. There were certainly several people there, perhaps up to a dozen. Powell, fiercely loyal to Booth, ignored the risk and agreed to proceed with the plan. David Herold also went along, as long as he did not have to kill anybody and could wait for Powell outside, holding their horses.

From the shadows, Powell and Herold watched Seward's doctors leave. The house was quiet now. They watched the gaslights go dim in several rooms, indicating that the occupants were settling in for the night. Powell handed his horse to Herold and walked across the street to the secretary's front door. He rang the bell. Herold scanned up and down the block as he stood watch, keeping their horses ready.

On the first floor of the house, a black servant named William Bell hurried to answer the door. Late-night callers, mostly messengers, were not unusual. There was no reason why the servant should not open that door.

Before him stood a tall, attractive, muscular man, well dressed in fine leather boots, black pants, jacket, and hat. He was holding a small package in his hands. The deception had worked. Nothing about Powell's appearance raised suspicion in William Bell. He greeted Powell and asked politely how he could help the visitor. Powell explained his mission: He was a messenger with medicine from Seward's doctor. That sounded reasonable. The servant reasoned the doctor must have prescribed some medicine and ordered it to be delivered to Seward immediately. Powell stepped into the hall and closed the door behind him. Bell reached out to accept the package. No, Powell said, the doctor said he had to deliver it personally to the secretary of state and instruct him how to take the medicine. The servant said he would take the delivery up himself. Powell insisted, "I must go up." He must see the secretary personally — those were his instructions. For five minutes, the assassin and the servant argued about whether Powell would leave the medicine with Bell. "I must go up," he repeated. "I must go up."

PAYNE, *alias* WOOD, *alias* HALL,
Arrested as one of the Associates of Booth in the Conspiracy.

Entered according to Act of Congress, by Alex. Gardner, in the year 1865, in the Clerk's Office of the District Court for the District of Columbia.

Lewis Thornton Powell, dressed in the clothing he wore the night he attacked Secretary of State William Seward; Powell operated under several aliases – Payne, Wood, and Hall.

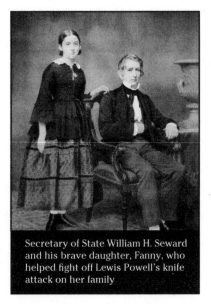

Secretary of State William H. Seward and his brave daughter, Fanny, who helped fight off Lewis Powell's knife attack on her family

DAVID E. HEROLD.

Entered according to Act of Congress, in the year 1865, by A. Gardner, in the Clerk's Office of the District Court for the District of Columbia.

David Herold, who accompanied Lewis Powell to Seward's home

Powell inched toward the staircase, backing Bell up to the landing. The servant was in grave danger now. Powell was almost out of patience. Powell lifted a foot to the first step, then another to the second. Bell chattered on, but Powell kept pounding up the stairs slowly, his boots striking the steps with dull thuds that echoed to the floors above. Luckily for Bell, he did not try to block Powell's path. Instead, he climbed the stairs with him.

At the top of the staircase, Seward's son Frederick confronted Bell and the stranger. Powell did not know it, but Frederick stood only a few feet from the closed door to the room where Secretary Seward lay. The stranger explained his mission again. Frederick explained that his father was asleep and that he would take delivery of the medicine for him. Again Powell refused, arguing that he must see the secretary. Incredibly, Powell, thanks to the little package he showed as a prop, had still not created suspicion about his true intentions. To Frederick, he seemed like a stupid and stubborn messenger.

From inside her father's bedroom, Fanny Seward sensed someone was in the hall. She hurried to the door and opened it only a little to shield her father from the bright gaslight from the hall. She saw her brother and the tall stranger in the hat and overcoat. She whispered, "Fred, Father is awake now." She knew in an instant she had done wrong. Powell leaned forward and tried to peek into the dark room, but Fanny held the door close, and the assassin was not able to see his target. He stared at Fanny and in a harsh and impatient tone demanded, "Is the secretary asleep?" Then Fanny made a terrible mistake. She glanced back into the room in the direction of her father, and replied, "Almost." Frederick Seward grabbed the door and shut it quickly.

It was too late. Innocently, Fanny had given Powell the information he desperately needed. Secretary of State William H. Seward was in that room, lying helpless in bed, defended by no one — Powell probably assumed — but a frail-looking girl. Powell did not know that Sergeant Robinson was in the bedroom, too.

Robinson, a wounded veteran, was serving as an army nurse, keeping watch over Seward as he recovered.

Frederick, still arguing with Powell, gave him an order: Surrender the medicine or take it back to the doctor. Powell glared, still refusing to give up his package. He finally pretended to give up, stuffed the package into his pocket, turned around, and started to walk down the stairs. He did not remove his hand from his pocket. William Bell, walking down ahead of Powell, looked ahead to the front door through which, in a few moments, he would take the ill-mannered visitor into the street. At the top of the stairs, Frederick Seward, satisfied at turning away an annoying pest, took his eyes off Powell and headed for his room. In an instant, Powell turned and rushed up the stairs. Before Frederick could turn around, Powell stood behind him. Seward whirled around, but too late: Powell was pointing a revolver at him, the muzzle inches from his face. In another moment, a .36-caliber bullet would explode in his face, and the hot black powder would, at such close range, not only kill him instantly but also burn his flesh a hideous black.

Powell, staring into Frederick's eyes, squeezed the trigger. The hammer fell and struck the percussion cap. Seward had no time to move — he knew he was dead. Then he heard . . . a metallic click. Misfire! The gun had not fired off its round! Frederick was still alive. But Powell, unlike his master, Booth, had five more rounds in his revolver. He could draw the hammer back with his thumb and take another shot. Then Powell made a mistake that jeopardized his mission. Instead of trying to fire again, Powell raised the pistol high in the air and brought down a crushing blow to Frederick's head. He hit him so hard that he broke the pistol, jamming the cylinder and making it impossible to fire the weapon again. In a fury, using all his strength, Powell clubbed Frederick Seward with the barrel of the broken revolver. William Bell ran down the stairs and into the street, shouting, "Murder!"

Watching from across the street, a nervous David Herold knew this was not part of the plan.

Fanny, unaware of the chaos on the other side of the door, sat in the chair beside her father. She heard the sounds of Frederick being beaten, and wondered what the noise was in the hallway. As soon as Sergeant Robinson

In this woodcut published by *Harper's Weekly*, Lewis Powell launches his attack on the household of Secretary of State Seward.

opened the door, Fanny saw a horrible sight — her brother's face, wild-eyed, covered with blood. Powell moved quickly. He shoved Frederick aside and struck Sergeant Robinson in the forehead hard with the knife, stunning him with the blow.

The assassin pushed past the stumbling sergeant and the frail girl blocking his path. He ran to Secretary Seward's bed, clutching the knife in his right hand and the pistol in his left.

In near darkness, Fanny raced Powell to her father's bed, trying in vain to throw her slender body between the huge assassin and her helpless father. The assassin reached the bed and pounced on Seward. "Don't kill him!" she shouted. Seward awoke, trying weakly to raise himself. He saw Fanny, then glimpsed Powell's unforgettable rugged face and burning eyes. The assassin pushed hard on the secretary's chest, pinning him to the bed. Powell used every ounce of strength he had to land a tremendous blow but, in the dark, missed twice. Determined not to miss again, he delivered a third mighty blow aimed at Seward's throat. The agonized groan that came from the bed told Powell that he had finally hit his target. The blade slashed open Seward's cheek so viciously that the skin hung from a flap, exposing his teeth and fractured jawbone. His cheek resembled a fish gill. Seward choked on the warm, metallic-tasting blood that spurted from his mouth and poured down his throat.

NATIONAL POLICE GAZETTE.

GEORGE W. MATSELL & CO.

NEW YORK: FOR THE WEEK ENDING APRIL 22, 1865.

VOL. XX. NO. 1025.—[PRICE TEN CENTS.

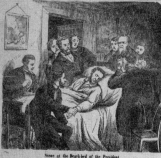

Scene at the Death-bed of the President.

Assassination of Abraham Lincoln, President of the United States.

Fight with the Assassin in Secretary Seward's Room.

Frederick Seward's Encounter with the Assassin.

The Assassination of Wm. H. Seward, Secretary of State.

John Wilkes Booth, the Assassin.

THE ASSASSIN'S CARNIVAL.

This action-packed April 22, 1865 issue of the National Police Gazette portrays scenes from what it calls "The Assassin's Carnival" — the assassination of Lincoln at Ford's Theatre, the attempted assassination of Secretary of State William H. Seward in his bed, and the

Across the room, Sergeant Robinson regained his senses. He would fight to the death before he allowed the assassin to murder the secretary and Miss Fanny. He charged into Powell. In an instant, the two battle-hardened Civil War veterans grappled in a death struggle. Powell's strength surprised Robinson — he could barely hold on to him as Powell went for Seward again.

Fanny screamed in an endless howling, terrifying wail that woke her brother Augustus, who was sleeping in a room nearby. She opened a window and screamed to the street below. That was enough to frighten David Herold into fleeing. He kicked his horse and fled, abandoning Lewis Powell. Powell kept fighting. Powell's experiences as a soldier would not permit one man and a screaming girl to scare him off.

Augustus Seward, dressed in his nightshirt, raced to his father's room and saw the shadows of two men fighting. Confused, he thought his father had become delirious and the male nurse, Sergeant Robinson, was trying to restrain him. As soon as he grabbed the shadowy figure he thought was his father, he knew it was someone else. Now combating two men, Powell fought harder, slashing wildly with the knife. He stabbed Robinson twice in the shoulder, deeply and to the bone. Robinson ignored the wounds and kept fighting. The sergeant and Augustus wrestled Powell into the hall and into the bright gaslight. Powell and Augustus, their faces inches apart, fixed their eyes on each other. Then Powell spoke. In an intense but calm voice, the assassin confided to Augustus, as though trying to persuade him, the strangest thing: "I'm mad. I'm mad!"

Powell wound his arm around Robinson's neck in a choke hold, and the sergeant braced himself for the knife that was sure to follow at any moment. Then, in a curious act of mercy, Powell let him go and, instead of stabbing him again, hit him with his fist. Powell fled down the stairs, out into the street, his eyes searching desperately for David Herold. He found nothing more than his lone horse. Powell tossed his knife to the ground, mounted his horse and, instead of galloping into the night, calmly trotted away. William Bell, waving his arms in the street, pursued Powell on foot for a few blocks, yelling all the way. Unable to keep up with the horse, he gave up and returned to the Seward house.

Fanny ran back to her father's room only to find the bed empty. She saw what she thought was no more than a pile of discarded bedsheets on the floor — but it was her father, in a bloody heap. To save his own life, he had rolled out of bed during the attack and crashed to the floor, hoping to escape Powell's reach in the dark room. Fanny slipped on a big puddle of blood and tumbled to the floor beside her father. He looked "ghastly . . . white, and very thin." And that made her scream, mistakenly: "O my God, Father's dead." Sergeant Robinson, ignoring his own wounds, lifted the injured Seward from the floor and laid him tenderly in his bed. Seward opened his eyes, looked up at his terrified daughter and, in unimaginable pain, spit the blood out of his mouth, and whispered, "I am not dead; send for a doctor, send for the police, close the house."

CHAPTER IV

Back at Ford's Theatre, the manhunt for Booth almost ended before it began when one man, an army major, rose from his front-row seat to pursue the assassin. The man, Joseph Stewart, long-legged at six foot five, decided to leap from the first row across the orchestra pit to the stage. In a few moments, he reached the stage and followed Booth into the wings. Stewart was the lone audience member who chased Booth.

Booth continued rushing through the wings of the stage and down the passageway leading to the back door that opened to the alley. A few more seconds and he would be in the saddle! The more immediate danger to Booth lay behind him. Stewart, following him down the passageway, was closing the distance between them with every stride.

Booth hoped that Ned Spangler or John Peanut stood on the other side of that door, still holding the rented horse. He burst through the alley door, sucked his lungs full of fresh air, and slammed it shut behind him. Booth spotted his horse standing quietly in the alley, just a few steps away. He eyed the man reclining on the bench near Ford's back wall and commanded, "Give me my horse, boy!" Booth pulled himself up onto the black-legged bay mare with a white star on her forehead and grabbed the reins. He balanced himself in the saddle. At that moment, Stewart swung open the theater door and saw Booth about to gallop away.

Stewart reached for the reins, but Booth, an experienced rider, spurred and pulled the horse in a tight circle away from Stewart. Stewart tried for the reins again, but Booth broke free and kicked the horse hard. The horse galloped down the alley, vanishing from sight.

Booth rode to F Street at the end of the alley. No one blocked his way. He entered F Street and turned right. He had escaped Ford's Theatre — barely. Could he escape Washington, its streets filled with thousands of soldiers and loyal citizens, all there to celebrate the end of the Civil War?

Booth rode past Herndon House, where just two hours ago he had met with his gang and dreamed of this moment. As he continued east on F, he approached two of Washington's greatest landmarks: to the left, the huge marble Patent Office. Just weeks ago, it had been the scene of Lincoln's inaugural ball. To the right was the massive

LEWIS C. PAYNE.

DAVID C. HAROLD.

THE SCENE OF THE GREAT TRAGEDY.

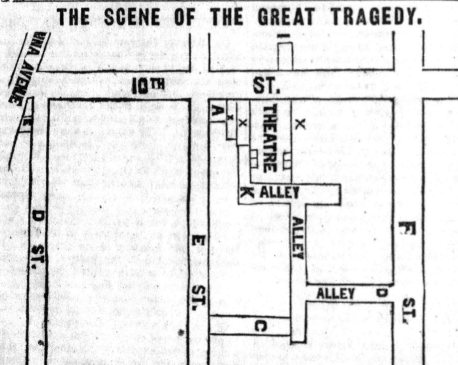

marble post office, where hours ago Henry Clay Ford had picked up the letter that he handed to Booth on the front steps of the theater. Gaslight bounced off the slick, polished walls of both buildings. Booth galloped past the buildings, onto Pennsylvania Avenue.

Few people saw him as he rode through downtown Washington. That was understandable, however, because Booth rode away from the crowds celebrating on Pennsylvania Avenue. Booth crossed the Capitol grounds, racing under the shadow of the great dome. He galloped toward the Navy Yard Bridge that led out of the city and into Maryland. Could he reach the bridge and cross it before pursuers or news of the assassination caught up with him? Luck was with him that night. His hard riding kept him ahead of the news. As he approached the river, he slowed his horse to a trot. He saw guards ahead. *Be natural,* he thought. *Don't arouse suspicion.*

Sergeant Silas T. Cobb was standing watch at the Washington side of the Navy Yard Bridge. He saw an approaching rider. He knew his orders: Allow no one to cross the bridge after dark. Cobb and the handful of men under his command prepared to challenge the rider. With the skill only an actor could manage under such stress, Booth prepared for a "performance" to talk his way across the bridge. The time was between 10:35 and 10:45 P.M.

"Who goes there?" Cobb challenged.

"A friend," the actor replied. Perhaps Cobb would recognize the star and wave him across with a smile? No such luck.

"Where are you from?"

"From the city," Booth replied.

Cobb asked his destination.

"I am going down home, down in Charles County."

The sergeant noticed that the horse was wet with sweat and had been ridden hard. Cobb continued to question Booth, asking if he knew that the bridge leaving Washington was closed at 9:00 P.M.

Booth claimed he did not know. He claimed that he had started out of the city late so that the rising moon would light his way.

Cobb reluctantly agreed to let Booth pass.

This was a lucky break for the assassin. If Cobb refused to let the actor cross the bridge, Booth had no other way out of the city. He could not turn back. He had to cross the river now, at this spot, into Maryland. Open, isolated countryside waited for him on the other side of the bridge. There he would be welcomed by friends. Armed with only a knife, he could not have fought the soldiers who blocked his way. Had Booth tried, the sergeant and his guards would have shot the actor out of his saddle and the manhunt would have ended then and there, less than an hour after Booth had assassinated Abraham Lincoln.

Once over the bridge, Booth turned to see if his hench-men — David Herold, Lewis Powell, or George Atzerodt — followed in the distance. This was their escape route, too. Booth saw no one, neither friends nor pursuers, behind him. From across the river, he saw a beautiful scene: a loom-ing moon, high over Washington, with the great dome glowing in the moonlight. He had done it. And he had escaped.

Booth and Powell had left behind so much blood. Blood-soaked, Sergeant Robinson and Fanny Seward worked to save Secretary Seward's life. Robinson showed Fanny the best way to slow the flow of blood from the wounds with cloths and water. If they could stop the bleeding until a doctor arrived, he might live.

Within minutes, messengers arrived with the doctors who relieved Fanny and Sergeant Robinson. The doctors confirmed that, despite their hideous appearance, the wounds were not fatal. To his doctors, Seward looked ghastly pale, corpselike, but he would live. One doctor treated the others Powell had so viciously attacked — Sergeant Robinson, Fanny, Augustus, and Frederick Seward.

As the night wore on, Fanny feared that Powell might return, or other assassins might be lurking in the house. Disobeying her mother, Fanny prowled from room to room, searching for hidden assassins. Finding none, she returned to her father's bedside and sat with him. Weakly, Seward reassured his brave girl that she had done well this night.

The Seward house grew quiet again. Everywhere she looked, Fanny saw signs of the horror that she and her family had just survived. She looked at herself: her hands, her arms, her long pretty dress, all drenched in blood. She could not stop screaming.

The president's box at Ford's Theatre was also drenched in blood. Mary Todd Lincoln stared at the president. He was still, his head hung low, his chin resting on his chest. She spoke to him, but he did not answer.

Clara Harris saw Henry Rathbone, wild-eyed, staggering, and clutching his left arm with his right hand. He could not stop the flow of blood flooding over his hand. Booth's knife had penetrated deep. Clara attended to her fiancé's wound.

Down in the audience, more than fifteen hundred people went wild. Some climbed to the stage, asking the occupants of the president's box what had happened. Hundreds of people turned to friends, spouses, and strangers to ask: "Has the president been shot?" "Who was that man onstage?" "Was that a knife?" "What did he say?" Half-crazed voices cried out demanding vengeance: "Kill the murderer!" "Hang him!" "Shoot him!" "Cut his heart out!" "Catch him!" "Don't let him escape!" None of them realized that the assassin was already out the back door. The mood inside Ford's became dark, ugly, and menacing. Under the dim glow of the gaslights, people fled in a panic. The voices grew louder until nearly all fifteen hundred of them created an angry roar. This was a mob!

Sitting just a few yards from the door to the president's box, Dr. Charles Leale jumped up from his seat. He made a direct run for the box — ignoring the aisles and jumping over chairs blocking his route. He struggled to get into the box through the door, which was barred by a piece of a wood blocking it. Leale, not in his Union uniform, announced his rank and profession. Major Rathbone, standing between Leale and Lincoln, asked the doctor to treat him first, holding up his injured left arm to show his wounds. Leale looked into Rathbone's eyes and, when he determined that the major was in no immediate danger, rushed to the president's side.

Dr. Leale introduced himself to Mary Todd Lincoln as a U.S. Army surgeon. He reassured her that he would do everything possible for her husband. As Mary wept, Leale began his examination of the president.

Lincoln looked dead. His eyes were closed, he was unconscious. Leale, remembering Booth's bloody dagger and recalling Major Rathbone's severely bleeding wound, assumed that Lincoln had been stabbed. Leale called for a knife. He had brought no surgeon's tools for a social night at the theater. If Lincoln had been stabbed, how could he stitch the wounds without needle and thread?

Leale was handed a pocketknife. He cut open Lincoln's

collar, shirt, and coat to examine him for knife wounds. There were none. Then Leale lifted the president's eyelids, studied the pupils and understood the seriousness of the wound: It was a brain injury. Leale weaved his hands gently through Lincoln's hair, and as he worked them thoroughly around the head, discovered that the hair was matted with blood. Leale's fingers probed for the source of the blood and found it behind the left ear: a neat, round hole, about the diameter of a man's fingertip, clotted with a plug of coagulated blood. Leale's heart sank.

He used his fingers to pull the blood clot from the bullet hole. That would relieve the pressure on Lincoln's brain. He dropped to his knees, straddled the president, opened his mouth, stuck two fingers down Lincoln's throat, and opened an airway. To draw life-sustaining oxygen into the lungs, Leale pressed Lincoln's chest and ordered two men to manipulate Lincoln's arms like levers on a water pump. He massaged the president's heart by pressing hard under the ribs. To everyone in the box, the situation seemed hopeless.

Then the president's heart began to beat and his lungs sucked in a breath. The heartbeat was weak, the breathing irregular, but Abraham Lincoln was still alive. Nevertheless, unless Dr. Leale could stabilize him immediately, Lincoln would die within a few minutes.

Leale leaned forward and breathed air from his own lungs directly into Lincoln's mouth and nostrils. Lincoln's breathing improved. Leale paused, studied his patient's face for a moment, and placed his ear over Lincoln's chest. Amid the shrieks, moans, cries, and Mary Todd Lincoln's deep sobs, he listened. The doctor leaned back and saw the president's lungs filling on their own. Quick action had saved the president from immediate death, on the floor of Ford's Theatre.

Still down on his knees, with all eyes fixed upon him, Dr. Leale announced his diagnosis and prediction: "His wound is mortal; it is impossible for him to recover."

Like Powell, on the night of April 14, George Atzerodt was armed with a knife and pistol — a six-shot revolver. His room at the Kirkwood House was one floor above Vice President Johnson's. Alone and unguarded, Johnson had gone to his room for the night. All Atzerodt had to do was knock on his door and the moment Johnson opened it, plunge the knife into his chest or shoot him dead. Compared with the challenges that faced Booth and Powell, Atzerodt had the easiest job of all.

But that night, Johnson escaped death. Atzerodt could not do it. He drank in the hotel lobby, and the more he drank, the worse the plan sounded. He did not knock on Andrew Johnson's door. He left the bar and walked out. Abandoning his mission, Atzerodt got on his horse and rode away. He wasn't sure what to do next. He was about to go on a rambling and error-filled escape journey.

In the saddle, a few blocks from Ford's, David Herold celebrated his escape from the Seward house disaster. He had gotten away just in time. No one in the house knew that Powell had an accomplice waiting in the wings. No one pursued him when he fled the scene and no one at the Seward house saw or could identify him.

He was safe for the moment. He was just another man on a horse on this night in Washington. He regretted abandoning his accomplice, but when he heard the screaming girl at the window, Herold decided to save himself.

Following Booth's escape route, Herold headed toward Maryland. He approached the bridge at Eleventh Street. Sergeant Cobb and his guards did not want to let another man pass. Cobb challenged him and asked where he was going.

"Home," Herold answered.

Cobb and Herold argued about whether he would be allowed to pass, in violation of the 9:00 P.M. curfew. Finally, without explanation, Sergeant Cobb waved Herold across the bridge.

Somewhere east of the Capitol building, Lewis Powell was not having as easy a time as Booth and Herold in fleeing the city. He had escaped Seward's servant and the others, and no one was chasing him now. But he did not know the city well. It got worse. He somehow lost or abandoned his surest and quickest means of escape from the city: the one-eyed horse Booth had bought. As midnight approached on the night of April 14, Lewis Powell was in trouble. He was a lone figure standing in the moonlight, lost, unarmed, and wearing a coat stained with blood. He did not know where he was, what to do, or where to go. For the next two nights, he slept in a tree. He began thinking of some of the places in Washington that Booth had taken him before. There was a boardinghouse, he recalled. He might be safe there — if he could just remember the address.

Thirteen miles southeast of Washington, John Lloyd, the proprietor of Surratt's tavern, went to bed. Although Mary Surratt had told him that afternoon to expect some nighttime callers, they had never shown up.

Several miles farther south, on an isolated farm near Bryantown, Maryland, Dr. Samuel A. Mudd, his wife, and their four young children were also in bed.

Abraham Lincoln slept, too. More than fifteen minutes after he was shot, he was still on the floor of the theater box at Ford's Theatre. Dr. Leale could not leave Lincoln to die on the floor of a theater, a place of amusement. As Leale considered his next move, a woman rushed through Ford's to get to the president. She knew history was being made in the presidential box and had convinced herself that she must be a part of it.

Actress Laura Keene's knowledge of the theater's layout enabled her to bypass the audience and crowds that stood between her and Abraham Lincoln. Still wearing her costume and carrying a pitcher of water that would serve as her passport to the president's box, she made her way up a hidden staircase that took her to a private office near the box. In less than a minute, she had crossed the theater and emerged on the second floor on the same side as Lincoln's box. She talked her way to the door, through the vestibule, and into the box. No one thought to prevent the great Laura Keene from entering the box.

The scene fascinated Laura Keene and stimulated her theatrical instincts. Hypnotized by the image of the fallen president, Keene imagined a scene with herself at the center of it. It was a once-in-a-lifetime chance, impossible for her to resist. Could she, the actress asked Dr. Leale, cradle the dying president's head in her lap? It was a shocking request and of no possible physical comfort or medical benefit to Lincoln, but Dr. Leale allowed it.

Laura Keene knelt beside Lincoln, lifted his head, and rested it in her lap. Bloodstains and tiny bits of gray matter from Lincoln's brain oozed on to the cream-colored silk fabric, spreading and adding color to the frock's bright and festive red, yellow, green, and blue floral pattern.

Laura Keene cherished the blood-and-brain speckled dress she wore this terrible night. In the days ahead, people begged to see the dress, to handle it and marvel at the stains on it. The dress vanished long ago, but miraculously a few small pieces — five treasured swatches — survived. Long ago the stains, once red, faded to a rust-colored pale brown.

She is remembered, not for her talent as an accomplished actress or her lifetime of performances onstage, but for the scene she staged in the president's box. Other great actresses from the nineteenth-century American theater have faded into oblivion while Laura Keene is remembered for a single unscripted act that took place over a few minutes in the box at Ford's on April 14, 1865.

The president of the United States could not die in a theater. Dr. Leale would see to it that Lincoln would die with dignity, in a proper bed. "Take him to the White House," someone begged. Impossible, Leale explained. Even the brief carriage ride between Ford's and the White House over unpaved, muddy streets, gouged with ruts and tracks from hundreds of carriage wheels, would be too much for Lincoln to endure. The bumpy ride would jostle the head wound and instantly kill him.

Leale and the others in the box prepared to move Lincoln's body without knowing where they would take him, just knowing that they must take him from that place.

Laura Keene's presence in the box brought attention to an uncomfortable fact. She was an actress, this was a theater, and it was Good Friday, the most solemn day on the Christian calendar. But the president of the United States was not worshiping in a church. Instead, he was dying on the floor of a theater, a place of entertainment.

Booth, now safely across the Navy Yard Bridge, rode into the dark. Of his three accomplices, he needed David

Herold the most. More than Powell or Atzerodt. Booth was a creature of the city and its fancy hotel lobbies, saloons, oyster bars, and gaslit shadows. He did not have the skills he would need to survive in the coming days, those of outdoorsman, hunter, or river boatman. But Herold was all of those things, and that's why Booth chose him, above all others, to be his guide.

Once Booth crossed the river into Maryland, he rode through a darkened and quiet countryside. Few travelers were using the empty roads. He trotted over the route he had rehearsed the previous year in preparing for the kidnapping plot. As Booth rode on, he searched the horizon for Soper's Hill, the chosen meeting place with Herold. In daylight, it was simple to find the place, but nightfall had obscured the hills. Alone in the country, he was out of his element.

Now Booth was more aware of the pain in his left leg. Near desperation after his hard ride, he glanced at the horizon. He was just beyond Washington's city limits. David and the others might be a few minutes ahead or behind him. Booth saw nothing ahead of him. When he turned to look behind him, he heard a noise in the distance: horses' hooves pounding the earth. Was it the first warning of a cavalry patrol in hot pursuit? As the noise grew louder, it sounded, to his relief, like one horse, not many. Then his pursuer came within sight — one small man on a gray horse. Relief trickled down the assassin's spine as he recognized David Herold. The actor was happy to be on safe ground, and now he had his guide.

Maryland, although it did not secede from the Union and join the Confederacy at the start of the Civil War, remained a hotbed of secessionists. Maryland was as Confederate as a state could be without actually seceding. If Maryland had seceded and become the twelfth star on the Confederate flag, the Union would have been in grave danger. The Union capital would have been completely surrounded by rebel states, isolated from the rest of the North.

Booth and Herold spurred their horses, riding southeast to their first safe house a few miles away. Booth probably peppered Herold with questions: Why is he alone? Where is Lewis Powell? Did Powell kill Seward? Did Atzerodt murder the vice president? Herold would have answered that he had not seen Atzerodt since the conspirators parted earlier in the evening to carry out the three assassinations. He had no idea whether Vice President Johnson was dead. Herold told Booth the details he knew of what had happened at the Seward residence: The trick of claiming Powell was a messenger from a doctor had worked perfectly. Herold heard no gunshots. About ten minutes after Powell entered the Seward mansion, a servant ran out the front door into the street screaming, "Murder!" And then a girl threw open an upstairs window and started yelling, too.

This news seemed to prove to Booth the faithful Powell had carried out his mission. But Booth must have been unhappy with Herold for abandoning Powell, whom he especially liked. And Powell would have come in handy if they had to do any fighting during their escape. Booth guessed that Powell, who had never learned his way around the capital city, was a lost man. Booth certainly told Herold of his success at Ford's Theatre. This was the assassin's first chance to describe his deed, and the actor in him probably made the most of the dramatic story.

Outside Ford's Theatre, bewildered pedestrians joined the crowd of theater patrons and hovered near the front doors awaiting the president. The public did not yet know whether Lincoln was still alive. Leale's team carried Lincoln through the lobby, out the doors, and across the steps where, just eleven hours earlier, John Wilkes Booth had sat reading his letter, calculating whether he would have time to put an assassination plan into action.

The crowd gasped when they saw Lincoln being carried out of the theater. They swarmed and surrounded the president. Leale, the doctors, and soldiers cradling the dying president halted. Where should they take Lincoln? Leale scanned the street for a refuge. Straining his voice to be heard by a sword-bearing officer, he shouted a command: Take the president straight across the street and into the nearest house. A soldier crossed ahead, pounding on the door, demanding entry.

In view of the horrified mob in the street, Dr. Leale pulled another blood clot from the hole in Lincoln's head to relieve the pressure on the brain and tossed the gooey mass into the street. Fresh blood and brain matter oozed through Leale's fingers.

When Leale was halfway across the street, soldiers on the other side yelled that the house was locked and no one answered the door. The scene was incredible, impossible! Stranded in the middle of the muddy street with no place to go, the president of the United States was dying in the presence of a mob of hundreds, perhaps a thousand, witnesses.

Until this moment, no one had paid attention to William Petersen's neat brick row house next door to the home that had been locked tight. It was a boardinghouse. Someone opened the front door of the house: A boarder had heard the shouting of the crowd and had gone outside to see what was happening. He stepped outside onto the top of the staircase and raised a candle. "Bring him in here!" he shouted above the sea of people. "Bring him in here!" Lincoln had found a safe house at last.

CHAPTER V

Riding in open country about ten miles south of Washington, John Wilkes Booth and David Herold would soon reach their own safe house. They did not expect any trouble along the road. They did not meet any soldiers as they rode toward Surratt's tavern. If they did, there was no danger because they were riding ahead of the news of the assassination. At this moment, Booth could safely ride past an entire regiment of Union cavalry. Not a soul in Maryland knew yet that Abraham Lincoln had been shot.

Within a few minutes of the assassination, the news began spreading, first by word of mouth from Ford's, then by messenger. It traveled no faster than a man could run on foot or ride on horseback. Between 10:30 and 11:00 P.M., more than fifteen hundred people spilled out from the theater onto the streets. They fanned out in all directions, like an unpaid army of newsboys shouting, "Extra!"

Block by block, they spread the news. Men ran or galloped to the White House, the War Department, and the homes of cabinet officers. They rushed home and wakened family members, knocked on neighbors' doors, roused children from their beds, spreading the news. Washingtonians were used to getting important news this way. Tonight, like an inferno burning outward in all directions from a single ignition point, the news that Lincoln had been shot spread from Ford's in an ever-widening circle.

A few blocks from Ford's, word of another apparent assassination spread from the Seward mansion and into the streets. Neighbors, soldiers, State Department employees, and even some reporters tried to enter the Seward house. Messengers fanned out in all directions shouting about the Seward assassination just as the news spread from Ford's of the president's assassination. It was only a matter of time before the two groups, bringing word of separate attacks, met in the streets. The same words were exchanged countless times that night: "No, I tell you it was Lincoln who was assassinated."

"Impossible, it was Seward. I just came from his house."

"And I just came from Ford's. It was Lincoln!"

"It was Seward!"

Then the terrible truth emerged: It was both.

Though unknown at the time, Seward still lived. Both men were attacked. The false information that Seward had been killed would continue to be spread through word of mouth.

At Thirteenth and K streets, someone rang the bell

at the home of Secretary of War Edwin M. Stanton. A brilliant man with a long record of public service, the president placed in his capable hands the most demanding tasks of the war: raising, training, equipping, and sending into battle the army of the Union. Creating that army was the largest organizational achievement in American history up to that time. Stanton weeded out unfit and incompetent officers; battled dishonest government contractors who sold the army low-quality uniforms, rotting equipment, and defective weapons; and endured an epidemic of officers who would not fight. If any man sat at Lincoln's right hand during the war, it was Edwin Stanton.

Stanton had been among those to turn down the president's invitation to join him and Mary at Ford's Theatre tonight. Instead, he left his office at the War Department and went home to dinner with his wife. Around 8:00 P.M., not long before the curtain rose at Ford's, Stanton left his house to visit his friend William H. Seward at his sickbed. Ever since the carriage accident Seward had suffered, Stanton had been a faithful visitor. He returned home about an hour later.

After he bid some visiting army officers good night, he closed his front door and locked it. It was 10:00 P.M. He walked upstairs and began undressing for bed. Not long after, the doorbell rang. His wife, still downstairs, unlocked and opened the door. If she had known about the murderous events of the evening, she most likely would not have opened the door. When she heard the (as it turned out, incorrect) news from the messenger, she shouted, "Mr. Seward is murdered!"

Her cry reached her husband upstairs, who did not believe what he heard. "Humbug," he shouted down. "I left him only an hour ago."

Stanton, still doubting, came downstairs. He found the messenger and several other agitated men. Alarmed by their manner and their story, he decided to ride over to the Seward home to investigate the rumor of Seward's death personally.

The ride to the Seward house took only a few minutes, and the first sign was not good. People filled the street and crowded around Seward's front door. An hour ago, when Stanton had left the Seward home, the street was deserted. Stanton arrived moments before Secretary of the Navy Gideon Welles reached Seward's house. A Navy Department messenger shouted unwelcome and, again, inaccurate news: President Lincoln has been shot, and Secretary Seward and his son Frederick have been assassinated.

Where, asked Welles, "was the president shot?" At Ford's Theatre, the messenger replied, adding that the Sewards had been attacked at home. "Damn the rebels," Welles cursed, "this is their work." He walked with the messenger to Seward's house.

Stanton, just behind Welles, charged up the stairs to Seward's bedroom. It was true! A scene of mayhem replaced the calm that Stanton had seen a little more than an hour before. The bed was saturated with blood. Several doctors hovered over the bloody secretary of state, working to save his life. Fanny Seward was wandering like a pale ghost, her dress dripping with blood. That was not all — Augustus Seward had been stabbed and his brother, Frederick, was unconscious from a crushed skull; brave Sergeant Robinson had endured multiple stab wounds.

Recovering from their initial shock, Stanton and Welles realized that there was nothing they could do for the victims: It was in the hands of the doctors and God. They turned their thoughts to the president and the rest of the cabinet. Stanton gave orders to rush military guards to the home of every member of the cabinet and to Vice President Johnson's hotel.

Without guards or army escort, despite the danger that might still lurk in Washington, Stanton and Welles rode in a carriage to Ford's Theatre. As the carriage clipped along, it passed men and women running crazily in all directions. The closer they got to Ford's, the thicker the crowds became. As the carriage turned down F Street, it approached a roaring, angry mob of thousands of people swarming in the street in front of Ford's.

On Tenth Street, Dr. Leale ordered Lincoln's bearers to head straight for the man with the candle standing at the top of the stairs at the Petersen house. The soldiers carried the president up the curved staircase. In this elevated position, the near-lifeless body of Abraham Lincoln became visible to the entire crowd gathered below. In awe, the people watched as their president disappeared into the board-inghouse. Except for a handful of doctors, government officials, and family friends who would enter the Petersen house, that glimpse of the president ascending the stairs was the last time Americans saw Abraham Lincoln alive.

Almost thirteen miles out of Washington, Booth and Herold approached their destination: Surrattsville, Maryland. The town was small, little more than a crossroads outpost, named after the family that owned the tavern there. Before they could continue on their escape south, the fugitives had business at the tavern. They would pick up the "shooting irons" Mary Surratt had ordered Mr. Lloyd to get ready that afternoon.

Surratt's place was hard to spot at night — the plain two-story structure was unpainted, and the dull wood boards reflected no moonlight. The tavern had served three functions: saloon, inn, and post office. In 1864, Mary Surratt, under a cloud of suspicion over her husband's loy-alty to the Union, had moved her family to her Washington, D.C., boardinghouse and rented the tavern to John Lloyd.

The tavern operated as a typical nineteenth-century roadside establishment. It was divided into private and pub-lic spaces. Paying customers entered, not through the front door, but through a side door that led directly into the bar and post office. The room smelled like wax, candles, oil lamps, tobacco, burning stove wood, whiskey, dirty clothes, and leather boots. Drink and meal prices were posted on a wall or chalked on a board. Nighttime callers were not unusual.

Booth and Herold rode their horses to the side entrance. The night was still. Inside, the tavern was quiet and dark. They had to make this quick. Herold dismounted and walked to the door while Booth remained in the saddle. They had no time to waste, and it would hurt Booth too much to dismount and put weight on his foot. Herold's pounding fist finally roused the innkeeper. John Lloyd climbed out of bed, went downstairs, and opened the side door. He recognized David Herold, a friend of John Surratt. Herold, impatient, hissed at him, "Lloyd, for God's sake, make haste and get those things."

Herold did not have to be more specific. Lloyd knew what they wanted. After Mary Surratt's afternoon visit, he took the "shooting irons" from their hiding place so they would be ready for the callers. Lloyd returned in a moment, bearing a small package wrapped in twine — the binoculars — and a loaded Spencer repeating carbine. Booth would further arm himself when he picked up pistols at his next stop.

As Herold and Booth prepared to ride away, Booth could not resist the temptation to brag. The impulsive actor had to tell someone of his achievement or he would burst! He told Lloyd, "I am pretty certain that we have assassinated the president and Secretary Seward."

Lloyd watched the pair ride off into the night, not understanding exactly what Booth had meant. He went back to bed. Booth and Herold had spent less than five minutes in Surrattsville.

They continued to the southeast for an unplanned but necessary detour. Booth's leg was throbbing painfully. He needed a doctor. And he knew just where to find one, four hours' ride away.

At the Petersen house, Abraham Lincoln would soon have more doctors than he could ever want, but little use for any of them.

Abraham Lincoln's body was carried into the dim hallway that led to the rear of the boardinghouse. As the bearers shuffled along through the tight passageway, they passed the parlors and stepped into the back room. The boarder who rented the room was out for the evening, celebrating the end of the war. Leale examined the small room with a bed, its headboard wedged into the corner. He glanced around the room. This place would have to do.

Chasing after the president, Mary Todd Lincoln, followed by Clara Harris and Major Rathbone, with Laura Keene trailing close behind, burst into the boardinghouse. Wringing her hands, Mrs. Lincoln pleaded, "Where is my husband? Where is my husband?" to no one in particular.

In the back bedroom, only one person mattered now. Someone tore back the bedding, someone else turned up the valve of the gas jet coming out of the wall. In an instant, the hissing, burning gas vapor lit the grotesque scene. The others laid the unconscious body across the mattress. Mary Todd Lincoln burst into the room, and the bright gaslight confirmed to her that this was not a nightmare as she hoped it was — this was real.

The air in the room was warm and moist, with too many people in it competing for the oxygen from the air. Leale ordered the windows opened and everyone but the doctors to leave the room. Mrs. Lincoln hovered over her husband. Leale gently encouraged her to leave the room and wait in the front parlor. Alone with their patient, the doctors worked quickly, removing the president's clothes.

Strangers slipped into the Petersen house before guards could be posted at the door. People invading the house inched their way down the hallway, closer to Lincoln. If someone did not take command of the situation soon, the house would be in chaos.

Stanton's carriage came to a stop, unable to get through the crowd. If they could not drive through, they would walk. On foot, in the dark, in the midst of thousands of people, anything could happen that night. Indeed, it already had. But now Stanton and Welles exited the carriage, headed into the mob, and vanished from sight.

The doctors examined Lincoln's body for knife or gunshot wounds but found nothing other than the bullet hole in his head. The president's feet and legs were already getting cold. The eyelids were so filled with blood that they looked bruised, like someone had punched the president in the face. All signs were consistent with a catastrophic injury to the brain. The surgeons covered Lincoln's body with a sheet and blankets. His breathing was regular but heavy, interrupted with an occasional sigh. They laid a clean white napkin over the bloodstains on the pillow. They placed a small chair at the head of the bed near Lincoln's face. Now the president was ready for Mary to see him again. Leale sent an officer to fetch her. She rushed into the room and sat beside her husband. "Love, live but for one moment to speak to me once — to speak to our children." Lincoln was deaf to her pleas.

With the president's medical condition stable for the moment, Dr. Leale sent messengers to fetch Robert Todd Lincoln, the president's eldest son, Surgeon General Joseph K. Barnes, Lincoln's family physician, another surgeon, and the president's pastor, the Reverend Dr. Phineas T. Gurley. Leale sent a hospital steward in search of a special piece of medical equipment, a Nelaton probe. There was work to do inside Lincoln's brain.

Ignoring the danger of the surging crowd, Stanton pushed through, up the stairs and into the back bedroom of the Petersen house. The sight of the president shocked him. He did not need doctors to tell him what would happen: Abraham Lincoln was going to die, and there was nothing the doctors could do about it. But he could do something for the president: He could protect and defend the country.

Stanton took charge, making the back parlor of the Petersen house his field office. He would not return to the War Department yet, but would remain here. Stanton believed that the Lincoln and Seward assassinations had exposed a Confederate plot to kill the leaders of the national government in an attempt to reverse the results of the Civil War. Stanton and his lieutenants assumed that all the cabinet heads had been marked for death that night. And a rebel army might be advancing on Washington at that moment!

Stanton wanted his commanding general, Ulysses S. Grant, back in Washington. He sent a telegram to order Grant back to Washington at once. It was the first telegram issued from the temporary War Department headquarters at the Petersen house. Stanton ordered troops to turn out into the streets, the guards to be doubled, military forts to be alert, guns manned, and special guards to be posted around the Old Capitol Prison. Clear away the mob from the street in front of the house, Stanton ordered. Soldiers tried to push back the crowd from around the foot of the staircase.

The immediate area secured, Stanton turned to his second mission, launching the investigation into the crimes that had occurred at Ford's and at the Seward house. He was determined to catch the criminals. He made it clear he was in charge. Later, when Vice President Johnson arrived at the deathbed, he remained in the background and chose not to take charge. In the days to follow, newly sworn-in President Johnson left it to Stanton to bring Lincoln's killer and his accomplices to justice.

Stanton had witnesses from Ford's Theatre brought before him. One witness after another swore it was Booth, John Wilkes Booth, who had shot the president.

Stanton's operators could wire news and orders all over the country — and soon telegraph lines across the nation were announcing the news: The president has been assassinated and the secretary of state attacked. Messages were telegraphed to Baltimore, New York, and beyond. Search the trains! Guard the bridges! Orders were sent to commanders in the field in Virginia, chasing down leads based on early but false information Stanton received from tipsters. In need of help, at 1:10 A.M. on April 15, Stanton sent a request to the chief of police in New York City, asking him to send his best detectives to assist in the investigation of the assassinations.

He continued to expand the search, activating manhunters in Delaware and Pennsylvania. Booth was identified to detectives as the assassin. Orders were sent to cover possible water escape routes. Cavalry rode to the Occoquan River to intercept anyone who attempted to cross. Fishermen along the river were notified to keep watch for Booth. The hunt had begun in earnest.

Back in Washington, Army Major General Halleck made plans to imprison the assassins when they were caught.

If Booth was captured, the army would have to protect him from Lincoln's avengers — rampaging mobs of vigilantes who might storm the Old Capitol Prison — if they discovered Booth was jailed there. It was too risky to imprison Booth anywhere on land. Halleck issued an order: If the assassins are caught, put them in double irons and take them to the commander of the Washington Navy Yard, who will confine them to a monitor warship anchored there. The river would protect Booth from the angry citizens of Washington.

Now all they had to do was catch John Wilkes Booth, Lewis Powell, John Surratt, David Herold, and George Atzerodt.

The doctors probed Lincoln's bullet wound with their bare, dirty fingers, sticking their pinkies inside Lincoln's brain. They used the Nelaton probe to find the bullet for possible removal, as if that would have helped Lincoln. Eventually, the physicians gave up their tinkering and simply monitored Lincoln's heartbeat, temperature, and breathing.

While Lincoln still lived, the manhunt was already under way. At Ford's Theatre, the Deringer pistol, the murder weapon, was recovered from the floor of the president's box. Soldiers and detectives rushed to Booth's room at the National Hotel. Of course, Booth was gone, but they searched his trunk and discovered an incredible and mysterious letter to Booth signed only "Sam" that described a large conspiracy against the Union government.

Several blocks from the National Hotel, just a few hours after the assassination, a group of detectives showed up at Mary Surratt's boardinghouse. In the chaos in the streets outside Ford's Theatre, one or more sources reported that John Wilkes Booth and John Surratt were close friends, and that Mrs. Surratt's boardinghouse was just a few blocks away. A boarder and school friend of John Surratt, Lewis Weichmann was the first to appear at the door to respond to the patrol's arrival.

The detectives announced their mission: They were there to search the house for John Wilkes Booth and John Surratt. Weichmann knocked on Mrs. Surratt's bedroom door, telling her that detectives had come to search the house. She instructed Weichmann to let them in. Weichmann seemed not to know why the house was being searched.

One detective revealed the shocking and half-false information to the occupants of Surratt's boardinghouse: "John Wilkes Booth has shot the president, and John Surratt has assassinated the secretary of state."

Weichmann told the detectives John Surratt was not at home, but in Canada, and offered to help them with their investigation. Mary Surratt claimed not to know where her son was. The detectives searched the house, then left, leaving Weichmann, Mary, and her daughter, Anna, behind.

Throughout the night and into the early morning, Mary Todd Lincoln made regular visits to her husband's bedside.

At one point, she wailed, "Oh! That my little Taddy might see his father before he died!" then fainted, falling to the floor. Stanton, startled by her cry, and fearing that the president had died, rushed into the room and called out loudly, "Take that woman out and do not let her in again." She did not deserve that cruelty. It did not matter: Stanton was obeyed.

After riding half the night on the deserted road south from Surrattsville, Booth and David Herold neared their destination — an isolated farmhouse a few miles north of a village called Bryantown. A city-dwelling night rider unfamiliar with the remote area might have missed the turnoff in the dark, but Booth rode confidently ahead. He had been here before. There appeared a handsome, two-story house in the distance. Booth recognized their sanctuary at once.

They could rest here. They would not be rushed, as they were at Surratt's tavern, which was much too close to Washington and possible pursuers. Here, farther south and in the darkness of this remote countryside, they could rest, eat, and sleep. And Booth could get medical care for his injured leg, which he was sure was broken. He needed to renew his strength after being awake for almost twenty-four hours. He was dog-tired, and his weary body ached from five bumpy hours on horseback.

The spring night air was still and eerily silent. Booth and Herold approached the farmhouse. No barking dogs warned of their arrival, and the slow pace of their horses' hooves failed to awaken the six people sleeping in the house.

Herold dismounted and walked to the house while Booth remained in his saddle. The assassin was alert for signs or sounds of danger. No lamplight shone through the window into the front yard. David would have to wake the people inside. He knocked on the door and waited for signs of life within the house. The loud rapping awoke the farmer, who was alarmed at being wakened in the middle of the night. The farmer rose from his bed, walked to the front door, and called "Who's there?" to the person on the other side. Two strangers, replied David Herold, on their way to Washington. One of their horses had fallen, he claimed, throwing the rider and breaking his leg. Hesitating, the farmer peered through a window, then unlocked the door.

In his front yard, he saw the two men about twenty feet away, standing under a cedar tree. He approached them. Booth relaxed at the sight of a familiar face. The farmer helped Booth dismount, offering support when the fugitive's body weight bore down on his injured leg. Booth grimaced in pain when his feet touched the ground. He staggered into the arms of Dr. Samuel A. Mudd.

Their faces only inches apart, Mudd helped Booth limp up the steps and into his home. Herold tended to the horses, then followed Booth and Dr. Mudd inside the farmhouse.

Dr. Samuel A. Mudd

Herold was a stranger to Mudd — the doctor had never laid eyes on him before — but Booth was not.

The chain of events that led John Wilkes Booth to Mudd's farm in the predawn hours of April 15, 1865, began six months earlier in Montreal, Canada. By late 1864, Booth had hatched the risky plan to kidnap President Lincoln. He attempted to recruit accomplices in New York City, a place where there were many Lincoln-haters and Confederate sympathizers. Booth knew the city well, of course. He had acted there many times.

North of New York, Canada was a major base of operations for the Confederate Secret Service. In Montreal, nests of rebel agents with plans and money were busy hatching anti-Union conspiracies. Booth sought contacts there. He and his little band of conspirators would snatch Lincoln and transport him out of Washington, south to Richmond. He needed no less than a rebel version of the Underground Railroad that transported runaway slaves north to freedom. Booth's railroad, however, would run in reverse. He would take the tyrant Lincoln, who had freed the slaves, south to the Confederate capital of Richmond. He would trade Lincoln for Confederate prisoners of war, or attempt to use his captive as leverage to give the South an advantage in peace negotiations. To pull off this plan, he needed loyal Confederate agents and safe houses located at points along the route.

One operative he met in Canada gave Booth letters of

introduction vouching for the actor's devotion to the Confederacy and requesting aid for him. One of the letters was addressed to Dr. Samuel A. Mudd.

Mudd, thirty-two years old, was a doctor living on a farm with his wife and family. He was anti-Union, anti-black, and the owner of up to eleven slaves before Lincoln's Emancipation Proclamation had freed them.

By November 9, 1864, Booth had visited the Bryantown tavern in southern Maryland. A combination saloon, inn, and post office — not unlike Surratt's tavern — it was known among Confederate sympathizers as a reliable safe house and place to exchange information.

A few days later, at church, Booth was introduced to Dr. Mudd.

In Maryland a month later, Booth again encountered Mudd at church. Booth invented a cover story. He claimed to be looking for real estate and a horse to buy. Booth needed horses for the kidnapping gang he hoped to put together. Samuel Mudd was happy to help. After church, Booth rode home with the doctor and spent the night at his farm. Mudd introduced Booth to a neighbor, who sold Booth a peculiar one-eyed horse.

Dr. Mudd had been helpful to Booth in Maryland, but the actor also needed the doctor's help — an introduction — in Washington. Mudd went to Washington to introduce Booth to a Confederate courier named John Harrison Surratt. Surratt operated out of his mother's boardinghouse on H Street and from her country tavern at Surrattsville. Booth would require the type of help Surratt could provide along his escape south.

On the way to the H Street boardinghouse, Booth and Mudd encountered John Surratt on the street and the introduction took place. Booth invited everyone — Mudd, Surratt, and Lewis Weichmann, a friend of Surratt's and a boarder at the H Street house — back to his room at the National Hotel for drinks and private conversation. Booth recruited Surratt into the conspiracy to kidnap the president, and soon became a frequent visitor to the boardinghouse, where he befriended Surratt's widowed mother and his young sister, Anna.

His work done, Mudd returned, just before Christmas 1864, to his farm and waited for further word from Booth about the kidnapping. No word ever came. Lincoln's second inauguration came and went in March. Richmond fell on April 3, Lee surrendered on April 9, but Dr. Mudd saw no more of Booth. Booth had sent liquor and supplies to Mudd's farm for hiding until the day came for Booth and his kidnap victim to flee the city, but it never did. Given the disastrous events of April 1865, Mudd assumed that the Union victory had changed the actor's plans and the scheme to kidnap the president had been abandoned.

Now, four months later, Booth was here at the farm again, though the doctor, standing in the darkness of his front yard, did not know it yet. Once inside, Booth sat on a sofa in the front parlor, then reclined. Mudd lit an oil lamp and dialed up the flame to permit a proper examination of his new patient. Their eyes locked in recognition; in an instant, the doctor knew the identity of the man who was lying in front of him. How could he fail to recognize the actor's familiar, thick black hair, pale complexion, trademark mustache, and striking good looks?

The first step in the examination process would be to pry the thigh-high cavalry boot off Booth's left leg. Mudd stood at one end of the sofa, took firm grip of the heel and sole, and tugged. Booth's jaw clamped tight in pain. The boot would not budge. The injury to Booth's leg had caused the tissue to swell up and create a seal that could not be broken without inflicting agony upon the patient and possibly worsening the injury. Mudd made a cut on the boot near the ankle, careful not to cut too deeply and open Booth's soft flesh. Mudd seized the boot firmly and pulled slowly. This time, it slipped off. He dropped the boot to the floor, removed Booth's sock, pushed his pant leg up his calf, and began the examination.

The diagnosis was simple: a broken fibula. Mudd informed Booth that he had a broken bone about two inches above the ankle joint. The doctor did not regard it as particularly dangerous or painful, reassuring Booth that he could treat the injury. He improvised a splint for Booth.

It was now about 5:00 A.M. Booth knew he should press

on south. He knew he was still traveling ahead of the news of the assassination, which Mudd was not yet aware of. He knew that news would spread and overtake him, making the daylight hours unsafe for traveling. Booth weighed the risk of capture against his desire for food and rest. No one in the world knew he had gone to Mudd's tonight. He had not known he would go there himself until after he shot Lincoln and injured his leg. Better to hide out and chance discovery than be caught in open country at sunrise. He and Herold would spend what few hours remained of this night at the farm, rest there all day, and then ride south at nightfall.

Mudd invited the pair to rest in his house for the night. He offered them a room upstairs and bade them good night. Unknown to Mudd, he had just extended his hospitality to Lincoln's assassin and his accomplice.

Their secret still safe from Mudd and his family, and their location a mystery to the manhunters, Herold and Booth collapsed into their beds. As Booth drifted off to sleep, he did not know whether his master plan had succeeded or failed. Had George Atzerodt and Lewis Powell carried out their missions and murdered Vice President Johnson and Secretary Seward? And what of the president — had Booth killed Abraham Lincoln, or did the tyrant still live? Booth did not know he would be damned in the morning newspapers as the most wanted man in America.

While Booth and Herold slept at the Mudd farmhouse, the first cavalry patrol rode south from Washington, headed for Maryland. Soon this group from the Thirteenth New York Cavalry, commanded by Lieutenant David Dana, would ride close to Mudd's farm. Booth had about seven hours.

CHAPTER VI

Edwin Stanton continued his investigation as Abraham Lincoln slept his last, deep sleep at the Petersen house. His brain was dead and beyond dreaming.

By 4:00 A.M., Stanton was sure that he was dealing with a conspiracy. The evidence found in Booth's hotel room included the mysterious "Sam" letter that seemed to predict the assassination. The recovery of this letter, which Booth had carelessly — perhaps on purpose? — let fall into the hands of the manhunters was obviously addressed to the actor by an unknown conspirator. Stanton read it and recognized that it was full of clues: Booth had at least two coconspirators named "Sam" and "Mike"; Sam was in Baltimore; the assassination was premeditated, planned before March 27; and the Confederacy might be involved.

At the Petersen house, a doctor recorded statistics in the notes he kept, tracking the sad and inevitable deterioration of Lincoln's condition that night.

5:50 A.M., respiration 28, and regular sleeping.

6:00 A.M., pulse failing, respiration 28.

6:30 A.M., still failing and labored breathing.

At the Petersen house, Abraham Lincoln began the death struggle.

The end was coming fast. Surgeon General Barnes placed his finger on the pulse in Lincoln's neck. Dr. Leale placed his finger on the pulse in Lincoln's wrist. Another doctor placed his hand over Lincoln's heart. The doctors and nearly every man in the room took watches out of their pockets. It was 7:20 A.M., April 15, 1865. More than once, they had thought Lincoln had passed away. But the strong body resisted death many times through the long night.

Abraham Lincoln took his last breath. His heart stopped beating at 7:22 and 10 seconds. It was over. "He is gone. He is dead," one of the doctors said. The occupants of the room stood silent and motionless for a few minutes. Edwin Stanton finally spoke. He asked Reverend Gurley, Lincoln's pastor, whether he would say a few words.

"I will speak to God," replied the minister. "Let us pray." He summoned up a very moving prayer, then murmured "Amen."

Stanton broke the long silence. "Now he belongs to the angels."

Stanton reached for pen and paper and wrote a single sentence. There was nothing else to say. It was the telegram that would transmit the sad news to the nation.

Washington City, April 15, 1865

Major General Dix,
New York:
    Abraham Lincoln died this morning at 22 minutes after 7 o'clock.

Edwin M. Stanton

Reverend Gurley and Lincoln's eldest son, Robert, told Mary the news. She would not go to the room where Lincoln had died. She could not bear it. She never saw her husband's face again.

Around 9:00 A.M., she left the Petersen house for the White House.

The room was empty of all visitors except Edwin Stanton. The morning light streaming through the back windows crossed Lincoln's still face. Stanton closed the blinds, took a small knife or pair of scissors from his pocket, and bent over Lincoln's body. Gently, he cut a generous lock of hair and sealed it in a plain white envelope. Stanton signed his name in ink on the envelope, then addressed the envelope TO MRS. WELLES. The memento was not for him but for Mary Jane Welles, wife of Secretary of the Navy

DAILY CITIZEN.
EXTRA.

ASSASSINATION
OF THE
PRESIDENT.

He was Shot at the THEATRE.

He Died at two minutes after 7, this morning.

THE NATION IN MOURNING

J. Wilkes BOOTH,
The Actor,
THE ASSASSIN.

ESCAPE OF THE ASSASIN!

DEATH OF SEC. SEWARD.

From the gentlemanly telegraphic operator, Mr. Mundy, we are able to lay before the public the mournful news of the assassination of the President of the United States.

We obtain from Quartermaster General Meigs the following account of the assassination:

"About half-past ten o'clock, a man dressed in a dark suit and ⟨illegible⟩ the private box, in which ⟨illegible⟩ and his party consisting of ⟨illegible⟩ Miss Harris, daughter of S⟨illegible⟩ and Capt. Rathbone, of ⟨illegible⟩ seated.

Immediately upon openin⟨g⟩ advanced toward Mr. Linc⟨oln⟩ barreled revolver in his rig⟨ht⟩ Bowie knife in his left. T⟨illegible⟩ who was intent upon the pl⟨ay⟩ tice his interruption, and t⟨illegible⟩ who was seated beside him ⟨illegible⟩ the reason of his entry. H⟨illegible⟩ time to ask the assassin wh⟨illegible⟩

he fired one charge from his revolver, which took effect in the back part of the President's head. The ball passed through and came out at the right temple. Capt Rathburn who was in the box with Mr. Lincoln attempted to arrest the murderer, and on so doing he received a shot in his arm. The assasin then leaped from the box to the stage. Before he disappeared behind the curtain he turned and with a tragic tone and flourish with his knite, shouted " Sye Semper Tyrannies."

So sudden was the affair, that for some moments after the occurrence, the audience supposed that it was part of the play, and were only undeceived by the manager announcing from the stage that President of the United States had been shot. The shock fell upon the audience like a thunder bolt, and loud cries were immediately raised to "kill or capture assassin."

The murderous emissary of the Slave power escaped easily and rapidly from the Theatre, mounted a horse and rode off.

The mass of evidence to-night is that J. Wilkes Booth committed the crime. Whoever it was, there are reasons for thinking that the same bold and bloody hand attempted the life of Mr. Seward.

The person who fired the pistol was a man about thiry years of age, about five feet nine inches high, spare built, fair skin, dark hair, apparently with large mustache.

Laura Keene and the leader of the orchestra, declare that they recognize him as J. Wilkes Booth, the actor and a rabid secessionist. Who ever he was, it is plainly evident that he thoroughly understood the theatre, and also the approaches and modes of escaping on the stage. A person not familiar with the

Gideon Welles and one of Mary Todd Lincoln's few friends in Washington. In 1862, she had helped nurse Willie Lincoln, ill with typhoid fever, until his death. Afterward, she did double duty, nursing Tad Lincoln and caring for Mrs. Lincoln, helpless in her grief. Shortly thereafter, the Welleses' own young son died of diphtheria. With that event, Mary Jane Welles and Mary Todd Lincoln shared a loss that brought them even closer to each other. Stanton knew that if any person in Washington deserved a precious lock of the martyr's hair, it was Mary Jane Welles. She later framed the cherished relic with dried flowers that had decorated Abraham Lincoln's coffin at the White House funeral. Stanton gazed down at his fallen chief and wept.

It was time to take Lincoln home. Stanton ordered soldiers to transport the president back to the Executive Mansion. The men arrived with a plain pine box. It looked like a shipping crate, not a proper coffin for a head of state. Lincoln would not have minded. He had always been a man of simple tastes. This was the plain coffin of a rail splitter.

The soldiers wrapped Lincoln in an American flag. They placed him in the box and screwed down the lid. The only sound in the room was the squeaking of the screws being tightened in the holes. The soldiers carried the coffin into the street and loaded it onto the back of a simple, horse-drawn wagon. The driver snapped the reins and the modest parade, escorted by a small group of bareheaded officers on foot, took Abraham Lincoln to the White House. There

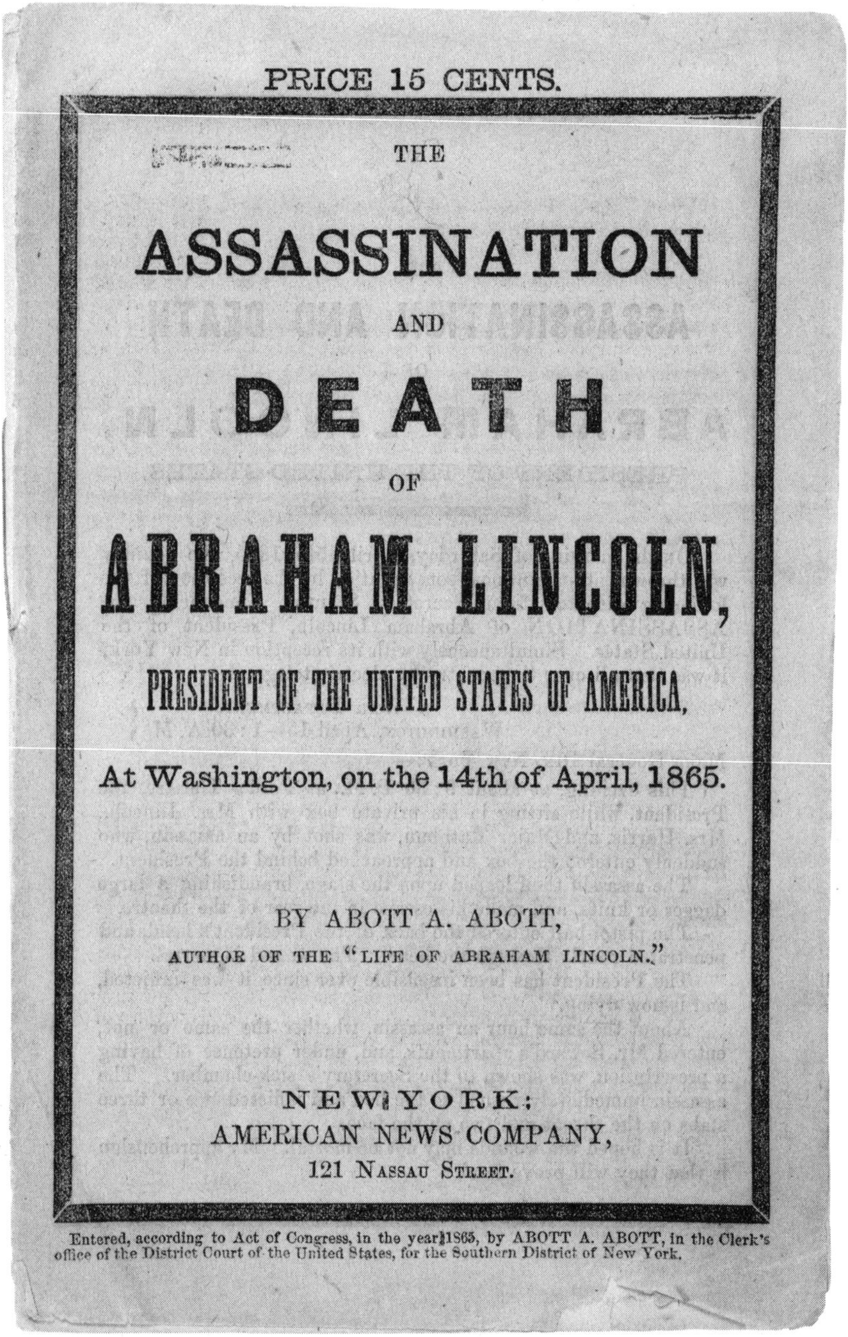

PRICE 15 CENTS.

THE

ASSASSINATION

AND

DEATH

OF

ABRAHAM LINCOLN,

PRESIDENT OF THE UNITED STATES OF AMERICA,

At Washington, on the 14th of April, 1865.

BY ABOTT A. ABOTT,

AUTHOR OF THE "LIFE OF ABRAHAM LINCOLN."

NEW YORK:
AMERICAN NEWS COMPANY,
121 NASSAU STREET.

Entered, according to Act of Congress, in the year 1865, by ABOTT A. ABOTT, in the Clerk's office of the District Court of the United States, for the Southern District of New York.

Soon after the nation's newspapers published the first accounts of the assassination and death of Lincoln, other publishers followed with pamphlets. This was the first.

were no bands, drums, or trumpets, just the beat of the hooves and the footsteps of the officers. Lincoln would have liked the simplicity.

Vice President Andrew Johnson was not present when Lincoln died, so the cabinet sent him an official notification of the president's death and of his succession to the presidency. Johnson agreed to take the oath of office at 11:00 A.M. in his hotel room at the Kirkwood House. Chief Justice of the Supreme Court Salmon Chase and the cabinet members found Johnson grave, dignified, and deeply moved. Given the tragic and unique circumstances of his elevation to the presidency, it was decided that it would not be appropriate for him to deliver a formal public inaugural address.

Though John Surratt was being sought by Stanton as one of Lincoln's assassins, he had not even been in Washington on April 14. Instead, he was in Elmira, in upstate New York.

The morning Lincoln died, John Surratt heard the news of Abraham Lincoln's assassination. Afraid that his name might be connected with Booth's, he fled to Canada. Then he decided that fleeing to Europe offered him the best chance of survival. In Rome, Italy, he joined the pope's army and eluded capture for a year.

In Maryland, Lieutenant David Dana of the Thirteenth New York Cavalry followed leads he received from informants. Unfortunately, he was pursuing the kind of false leads that would come to haunt the manhunters in the days ahead.

Little more than an hour before Lincoln died, George Atzerodt rose from his humble room at the Pennsylvania House and left the hotel. As Atzerodt walked along Booth's escape route just two blocks from Ford's Theatre, he tossed his knife under a wood carriage step, into the gutter. A few minutes later, a sharp-eyed woman looking out a third-story window in a building across the street saw it there. The clue, still in its sheath, was taken to the chief of police.

From New York City came an offer of help, twelve hours after Stanton had asked its chief of police to send his finest detectives to Washington to help track the president's killer. Stanton also summoned Lieutenant Lafayette C. Baker, one of his favorites, to leave New York for Washington.

The executive branch of the government — Vice President Johnson and the cabinet — had survived the night; no other assassinations had occurred. No invading rebel army stormed the capital. Secretary Stanton attempted to coordinate the efforts of the local police force, detectives, and the army. Booth and his conspirators had to be caught before they vanished into the Deep South, where they would find aid and comfort in the heart of the Confederacy.

At the farm, Dr. Mudd's wife, Frances, rose early, called for her servants to prepare breakfast, and woke her husband. After only two hours of sleep, David Herold walked downstairs and joined the Mudds for breakfast while a servant carried breakfast upstairs for Booth. Booth, his mind and body still exhausted from his great day, stayed in bed. He was too far from Washington to hear the ringing bells of the city's churches tolling in mourning.

As he made casual conversation at the breakfast table, Herold appeared unaware of the danger he faced. He was running for his life, but seemed to the Mudds not to have a care in the world. He asked for a razor so that he could shave, and asked Dr. Mudd if he would make a pair of crutches for Booth. Mudd fashioned a crude pair out of a piece of plank and sent them up to Booth.

By 8:00 A.M., George Atzerodt had walked to Georgetown, on the way to his cousin's house. He showed up at Matthews & Co.'s store and paid a call on an acquaintance. He tried to raise some money: first by selling his watch, then by using his revolver as collateral for a ten-dollar loan. Atzerodt left the store with the money and continued his journey. He would leave Washington. He knew a place where he thought he would be safe.

At the Executive Mansion, the soldiers carried the president's body in its temporary coffin to the second floor for an autopsy. Cutting open Abraham Lincoln's brain and body served little scientific purpose. The surgeons already knew what had killed him — a single bullet through the brain. They hid their morbid curiosity behind the shield of scientific investigation. One surgeon reached for his saws and knives while the others watched. And they wanted the bullet. The nation could hardly bury its martyred Father

Abraham with a lead ball lodged in his brain. They cut it out, marked it as evidence, and preserved it for history. His blood, according to a newspaper report, was drained from his corpse by an embalmer, transferred to glass jars, and preserved. When they were finished, Mary Todd Lincoln sent a request: Please cut off a lock of his hair for her.

With Dr. Mudd providing advice and assistance, Herold rode to Bryantown to find a buggy or carriage to transport Booth south. When they got within sight of the edge of town, Herold yanked back hard on the reins and brought his horse to a stop. He could not believe what he saw several hundred yards ahead. Mounted men, wearing a uniform Herold recognized: Yankee cavalry! Manhunters!

Herold had just spotted the Thirteenth New York Cavalry. Lieutenant Dana had led his troops into Bryantown, a well-known place of Confederate intrigue, commandeered the tavern, and occupied the town. Dana intended to establish a command center there, and from Bryantown launch cavalry patrols through the surrounding countryside, in pursuit of the Lincoln and Seward assassins. They were just a few miles from Mudd's farm. This was the closest the pursuers had gotten to Booth since the assassination.

Herold made a quick decision to get out of Bryantown before he could be spotted by the cavalry. He told Mudd he didn't need a carriage after all, Booth could still ride a horse. Mudd was puzzled by the sudden change in plan, as Booth had not yet told Mudd he was Lincoln's assassin. Mudd continued into Bryantown at a relaxed pace, just as he had done on countless Saturday afternoons.

He went about his business, buying supplies, greeting friends and neighbors he passed in the streets. But a strange, wild atmosphere hung over Bryantown. The cavalrymen's faces were angry. Mudd wondered what had happened. Then someone blurted it out: Abraham Lincoln had been assassinated in Washington last night! He died early this morning. The cavalry is here in pursuit of the assassin who escaped. Detectives and soldiers were searching the Maryland countryside, hunting the murderer. Most astonishing of all was who had done it. It was the actor John Wilkes Booth!

Mudd remained calm and did not betray the secret known, at this moment, to him alone: America's most wanted man was hiding in a farmhouse, less than five miles away!

Herold rode to the farm to warn Booth. When he arrived, Booth was still in bed, but he wouldn't be for long. The cavalry is here, Herold warned. They are just down the road in Bryantown.

It was around 3:00 P.M., Saturday, April 15, and Booth was in grave danger. Only Samuel Mudd stood between him and disaster. Mudd had the power to end the manhunt for Lincoln's killer that afternoon. All he had to do was tell the soldiers that John Wilkes Booth and his accomplice were hiding at his farm. He could tell them Booth had a broken leg; he cannot run away. He could take them to Booth right now. All he had to do was tell them, and Dr. Samuel A. Mudd would become, instantly, a national hero.

Booth faced the difficult choice of what to do next. If the doctor had betrayed him to the troops in Bryantown, Booth was a dead man. If they did not kill him on the spot at Mudd's farm, then they would escort their captured prey back to Washington for a hanging. Instead of fleeing the farm immediately, they waited for the doctor's return.

After 6:00 P.M., Mudd finally rode down the main road and made the turn toward the farm. He was alone and brought no cavalry. Booth's judgment of Mudd's character had been correct: He had not betrayed them.

Mudd could not hide his distress. He ordered Booth and Herold to leave his farm at once. Ignoring Mudd's anger, Booth focused on the priceless news the doctor had brought back from Bryantown. The president was dead, and the fame was his! Less than twenty-four hours after the assassination, Dr. Mudd had just given Booth the first confirmation that he had killed Lincoln!

Booth might rejoice at the news of the tyrant's death, but Mudd was angry and afraid. By coming there, Booth had placed Mudd and his entire family in great danger. Yes, Mudd had agreed to help Booth with the kidnapping of Abraham Lincoln, but no one had consulted him about murder! Now, by offering Booth his hospitality, he had unknowingly made himself an accomplice in the most shocking crime in all of American history — the murder of the president of the United States!

Mudd continued to insist that Booth and Herold leave his farm at once. But he was sympathetic to the assassin's situation. He was no fan of Abraham Lincoln, the Union, or black people. Booth may have involved him and abused his hospitality, but not enough to make Mudd betray him. Mudd agreed that, as long as they left immediately, he would still help the assassins.

He would not return to Bryantown and report Booth's whereabouts. He would hold his tongue and allow Booth a head start. If the soldiers came to question him, he would say only that two strangers in need of medical assistance stopped briefly at his farm. Then he would send the man-hunters in the wrong direction.

Mudd gave Booth the names of two trustworthy local Confederate operatives, William Burtles and Captain Samuel Cox. Then Mudd explained the route to the next stop on their underground rebel railroad. They must travel south-east in a wide arc to avoid the troops in Bryantown. About two miles south, they would find the Burtles place. Cox's farm was several miles further southwest, and from there they would be close to the Potomac River. Mudd also gave Booth the name of a doctor on the Virginia side in case his leg continued to trouble him.

David helped Booth climb onto his horse and handed

him the crude crutches Mudd had made for him. Mudd, relieved by their leaving, watched them ride off until they vanished from sight.

It was around 7:00 P.M., fifteen hours since the assassins had arrived at Mudd's door, and just under twenty hours since John Wilkes Booth had shot the president. As dusk faded to dark, Booth and Herold continued south, careful to watch for signs of cavalry. The pair had a long night's ride ahead of them. But they had survived the first day undetected.

Although Dr. Mudd had shown Booth the route they must take, Booth and Herold got lost. They were fortunate to come upon a local man, Oswell Swann, half black, half Piscataway, who, for seven dollars, agreed to take them directly to Captain Cox's place. Oswell Swann earned his pay this night. He guided them safely through the Zekiah swamp, with its muck, snakes, and wild, overgrown vegetation, to the doorstep of Captain Samuel Cox. It was after midnight April 16, Easter Sunday.

CHAPTER VII

Back at Ford's Theatre, the investigation was well under way. Stanton was determined to preserve the scene of the crime. He ordered the theater to be surrounded by a twenty-four-hour guard. He wanted photographs of the interior of the theater, to record exactly how it appeared at the moment of the assassination. Matthew Brady, who had photographed Lincoln many times, now photographed the scene of his murder. He captured the stage and its scenery as it was at the time of the assassination, the exterior of the president's box, the approach to the box, and the outer door leading to the vestibule.

Easter Sunday 1865 would forever be known as Black Easter to those who lived through it. Abraham Lincoln's murder transformed a time of rejoicing in the capital to a time of mourning. Across the country, ministers stayed up late Saturday night and by candle or lamp wrote out the final words of sermons they began composing as soon as they heard the terrible news of the president's death.

In the early hours of Black Easter, Booth and Herold sought their salvation: not in a church, but at the door of a loyal Confederate. At the Cox house, Herold dismounted and knocked. Booth stayed on his horse under the cover of a tree in the yard. Cox poked his head out from a second-story window and asked, "Who's there?" Herold refused to give his name, not sure if he could trust the captain. He said only that he was with a man who needed help.

Suspicious, Cox opened the door and looked over the worn-out, crazy-eyed man standing before him. The stranger seemed more like a boy than a man. The farmer looked around his yard. Booth dismounted with some difficulty and hobbled up the porch to the door. In great pain, he pleaded with Cox for help. It was there, by brilliant moonlight, that Cox saw the initials J.W.B. tattooed on the hand of the injured stranger. It was there the sweet-talking actor used his charms and talents to win over the man to his cause. Cox swung open the door and invited the fugitives into his home. To the nation, Black Easter dawned as a day of great mourning; to John Wilkes Booth, it began as a day of salvation.

Precisely what Booth told Cox on the front porch — and during the next few hours they spent together in the house — remains a mystery. The assassin of the president was in there, injured, desperate, and on the run from a manhunt. Given the unusual things Cox and his son were about to do for Booth, given Booth's state of mind, there is little doubt that Booth confessed all to his hosts. Father and son saw the murderer and his accomplice and decided to help them. Cox helped them decide on their next move. He told Booth there was only one man who could get them safely across the Potomac River. That man was Thomas Jones.

They would summon Thomas Jones after sunrise the next morning. For now, it was too dangerous for Booth and Herold to remain at Cox's farm. Instead, they would hide in a heavily wooded pine thicket some distance away. No one would search for them there, Cox reassured them, and it was unlikely any locals would happen to see them there. They were not to build a fire — someone might see it. In the morning, someone would come to them. That person would signal with a specific three-note whistle as he approached. They were to beware anyone who did not make that sound.

Booth and Herold ate the food Cox offered them, saddled up for the ride to the pine thicket, and rode off with Cox's overseer as their guide. If their luck held, they would cross into Virginia sometime after nightfall, within twenty-four hours. If, that is, they could survive just one more day in Maryland.

Booth and Herold entered the pines, dismounted, and tied off their horses. Exhausted, the two men unrolled their blankets on the damp earth, laid down, and gazed up at the immense black sky decorated by countless points of twinkling light. It would be morning in a few hours. If Captain Cox's word was true, it was safe to doze off until then.

The rising sun and chirping birds woke Booth and Herold early in the morning. Now they could do nothing but wait. Back at the farm, Captain Cox had to find out whether his friend would actually help Booth and Herold. He sent his son to fetch Thomas Jones right away.

Thomas Jones was a Confederate Secret Service veteran who had spent his entire life trailblazing through the fields, thickets, and forests of rural Maryland and navigating its streams, marshes, and rivers. During the war, he had ferried hundreds of men, and the occasional female spy, across the Potomac River between Maryland and Virginia. He transported the Confederate mail between the two states and sent south fresh Union newspapers that provided information valuable to the Confederacy. Jones was a valuable and mysterious secret agent operating along the watery borders between Union and Confederate territory. The Union army had never caught him in action — he was a river ghost to the boys in blue uniforms. His knowledge of the river enabled him to calculate the best time to begin a trip across. They should leave a little before sunset, when the reflection in the water of the high bluffs near Pope's Creek extended out into the Potomac until it nearly met the shadows cast by the Virginia woods. It would be difficult to spot a small rowboat floating in the river.

Jones's service to the Confederacy had cost him a great deal. Suspected of disloyalty to the Union, federal forces arrested and jailed him for months at the Old Capitol Prison in Washington. When Jones went to the Confederate capital, Richmond, at the beginning of April 1865 to collect the money owed him by the Confederacy, he discovered that the army had evacuated the city and he went unpaid. He lost $2,300 owed to him for three years of service, along with all the money he had invested in Confederate bonds at the beginning of the war. All this meant Jones needed as much money as he could lay his hands on.

At Jones's farm, the Cox boy told Jones his father wished to see him at once. "Some strangers were at our house last night," the boy said. Jones's eyes lit up. Could he mean the heroes who assassinated President Lincoln? The report excited Jones. The day before Jones learned from Union soldiers that Lincoln had been assassinated, and they had information that the assassins had traveled this way. Jones felt it in his bones: Captain Cox wanted to see him about something connected to the assassination!

Jones saddled up and accompanied young Cox to his father's farm. Once he arrived, Captain Cox and Thomas Jones spoke casually for a few minutes until Cox could avoid the subject no longer.

"Tom, I had visitors about four o'clock this morning,"

Cox revealed. "They want to get across the river." He spoke in a whisper. "Have you heard that Lincoln was killed Friday night?"

Yes, Jones replied, telling Cox about what he had learned about the assassination from the Union soldiers.

Cox finally blurted out, "Tom, we must get those men who were here this morning across the river." Then he told Jones everything about the late-night visit from Booth and Herold.

Jones was no coward. Four years of loyal, dangerous service to the Confederacy had proved that. But the war was over. Jones considered the situation. Then he made up his mind. "I will see what I can do," he said. "I must see these men; where are they?"

Captain Cox told Thomas Jones that Booth and Herold had spent the night in the pine thicket. Lincoln's killer was there now, waiting for someone to rescue him. Cox gave Jones the whistle code — a set of three notes — and cautioned him to approach the fugitives carefully. "They are fully armed and might shoot you through mistake," he warned.

Alone, Jones rode toward his meeting with Lincoln's assassins. At the edge of the thicket, he stopped, whistled the three notes, and waited. David Herold rose from the brush and aimed his Spencer carbine at him. The weapon was cocked and ready to fire. "Who are you, and what do you want?" demanded Herold.

Jones told Herold that Cox had sent him, and that he

was a friend. Herold relaxed his grip on his gun and said, "Follow me." He took Jones deeper into the pines, through thick undergrowth, to a man partly concealed by the brush. Jones, overcome by a mixture of thrill and fear, saw John Wilkes Booth for the first time. He later recalled that Booth was dressed in stained, dark clothes. Booth was very pale and his face bore signs of suffering.

Booth confided what Jones already knew: Booth had killed Lincoln. The assassin understood that the odds of escape were against him. He also vowed that he would never be taken alive. Jones was sure he meant it.

Jones proposed a plan. He would help Booth and Herold cross the Potomac River to Virginia, but they must leave it to him to decide when and how they would make the attempt. Patience was essential. Meanwhile, Jones would feed them and make preparations for their crossing.

Booth and Herold must not leave the pine thicket, make any noise, or do anything that might let anyone know they were there. Jones said that to cross the river they needed a dark night, smooth water, and deserted riverbanks. It would be best to wait for the departure of many of the soldiers and detectives who had already followed Booth south into Maryland. That might take days. And there would be no doctor for Booth until they crossed the river.

Jones persuaded the assassins that the best way to escape was to stop running and go into hiding. Manhunters were already nearby. Soon federal forces would join Lieutenant

Dana and fan out across the part of Maryland Booth and Herold were in. They would remain in hiding and let the manhunters sweep through the county before they moved on.

Booth's curiosity about public reaction to the assassination led him to make an additional request of Jones: Please bring some current Washington newspapers from the day Lincoln died or from today, the sixteenth. Despite his pain and exhaustion, the actor was eager to read about his deed in the papers.

Jones mounted his horse, maneuvered through the pine trees, and vanished from sight. Until Jones returned, Booth and Herold were on their own.

With his simple plan, Jones foiled the whole manhunt for John Wilkes Booth. A single Confederate agent, nearly penniless, had just frustrated the frantic pursuit by thousands of men being directed from Washington by Secretary of War Stanton.

Late on Easter morning, George Atzerodt showed up at the home of Hezekiah Metz, about twenty-two miles from Washington, in Montgomery County, Maryland, north of Charles County where Booth and Herold were. Atzerodt joined Metz and three of his guests for a midday meal. One of the guests had known him for years, and when Atzerodt arrived he teased him.

"Are you the man that killed Abe Lincoln?" The joke must have frozen Atzerodt in his tracks. Atzerodt laughed

THE NEW YORK HERALD.

WHOLE NO. 10,457.　　　NEW YORK, SUNDAY, APRIL 16, 1865.　　　PRICE FIVE CENTS.

OUR LOSS.

The Great National Calamity.

DEATH

OF THE

PRESIDENT.

Sad Details of the Terrible Event.

The Last Moments of the President.

SCENE AT THE DEATH BED.

The Life and Services of Mr. Lincoln.

IDENTIFICATION OF THE MURDERER.

John Wilkes Booth the Assassin.

Secretary Seward Thought to be Out of Danger.

FREDERICK SEWARD NO BETTER.

THE METROPOLIS IN MOURNING.

THE EXCITEMENT.

MEETING IN WALL STREET.

Speeches of Generals Butler and Garnedts, Daniel S. Dickinson and Others.

ALL THEATRES CLOSED.

THE GRIEF OF THE NATION.

Business Suspended Throughout the Country.

THE NEW GOVERNMENT.

Inauguration of Andrew Johnson as President.

The Policy of Mr. Lincoln to be the Policy of Mr. Johnson.

THE CABINET UNCHANGED.

SKETCH OF MR. JOHNSON.

HIS LAST SPEECH.

The Return of General Grant to Washington,

&c.,　　&c.,　　&c.

DETAILS OF THE CALAMITY.

THE HERALD DESPATCHES.

The April 16 issue of the *New York Herald* confirmed the death of the president.

and said, "Yes." He also confirmed for the guests that Seward's throat had been cut, his sons attacked. Atzerodt, the slow-witted German, did not know it, but he had just sealed his fate. One of the guests would inform the local authorities of Atzerodt's boast.

After dinner, Atzerodt, unaware that he had aroused the suspicions of the guest, traveled to the home of his cousin Hartman Richter, arriving after 2:00 P.M.

That day, Samuel Mudd considered his situation. At some point, probably soon, the soldiers or detectives would discover two things about him: He had visitors on assassination night and, even more damning, he had known ties to Booth. He did not wish to betray Booth, but too many people at Mudd's farm had seen Booth and Herold for Mudd to keep the visit a secret forever.

Mudd solved his problem by sending his cousin George, a loyal Unionist and therefore above suspicion by the federal authorities, to town to report Booth's visit to Mudd's farm. The vague, secondhand report he would deliver would not likely cause the soldiers to leap into their saddles in pursuit of the two strangers. Through the afternoon and into the evening, Dr. Mudd awaited the arrival of the manhunters. But they did not come. In a stroke of good luck for Booth, for unknown reasons Samuel Mudd's cousin George failed to ride into town to report the strangers to the cavalry. The delay gave Booth an additional lead over his pursuers.

In Washington, the manhunt had progressed little. John Wilkes Booth had assassinated the president almost forty-eight hours before, but the manhunters had no solid leads. Yes, the police, detectives, and officers had found a number of leads on Booth's accomplices, but none led to Booth.

Hats, the Deringer pistol, abandoned knives, broken revolvers, jackets, one-eyed horses, bankbooks, mysterious letters, hotel registers, notes to vice presidents, trunks, rope, spurs, bridles, saddles, and eyewitness accounts were all fine clues that made the assassin seem very vivid and near. These would make good evidence at a criminal trial as proof of identity and guilt. The evidence already collected by April 15 confirmed that it was Booth who had shot Lincoln, and that he seemed to have several accomplices. The contents of Atzerodt's room at the Kirkwood, plus Booth's "Sam" letter, suggested that the vice president had also been marked for death. The evidence pointed to Booth's guilt, but not to how he planned to make his escape. Booth could be any-where. Many false sightings across the country made the pursuit more difficult. With each passing hour, Booth's trail grew a little colder. Soon he would disappear forever. Booth's skill at avoiding the manhunters increased the government's embarrassment over its failure to find him.

On the night of April 16, Stanton had no idea of John Wilkes Booth's location or destination. Yes, it was proba-bly Booth who gave the name *Booth* to Sergeant Cobb at the bridge and fled into Maryland. But where did he go after that?

On Monday, April 17, Thomas Jones appeared to go about his business as usual. He did his chores and ate his usual breakfast. He grabbed some bread, butter, and ham, filled a flask with coffee, and stuffed everything into his pockets. He folded the newspapers and stashed them in his coat. He carried a basket of corn on his arm to throw off any Union troops he might encounter. If stopped and questioned, he could claim that he was on his way to feed his hogs, which ran free in the woods. A little before 10:00 A.M., Jones rode toward the pine thicket.

About a hundred yards from Booth's camp, Jones dismounted, walked slowly, and whistled the secret signal as he came within earshot of the assassins. Booth and Herold welcomed him, and the food he brought, with open arms. Booth was especially eager to see the other treats Jones brought — the newspapers! At last, three long days after the assassination, he could read about his history-making actions and how they were reported to the nation. He must have delighted in reading the details of the assassination as reported in the papers, as though reading the reviews of a performance.

Booth's pleasure at reading about his success in killing Lincoln could not hide his worsening condition. His leg was in bad shape, and Booth was obviously in great pain. As Jones discussed the escape plan with Booth and Herold, he became distracted when he heard a familiar and terrifying sound in the distance — clanking metal and horses' hooves pounding the earth. Instantly, Jones recognized the sound — cavalry sabers slapping the saddles of Union troops riding in their direction.

It was too late for them to try to hoist Booth onto a saddle to attempt escape. A fight was out of the question: Booth could not walk, Jones was unarmed, and Herold had never been in a battle before. With only two revolvers and one carbine, they couldn't hold off a patrol of Union cavalry for long. The three men hugged the ground and held their breath. The cavalry horses got within two hundred yards. It was Booth's closest brush with capture since he galloped down the alley behind Ford's Theatre. Lucky for Booth, instead of turning into the thicket, the troops remained on the road, passed the thicket, and rode until the sound of hoofbeats vanished in the distance.

Jones locked eyes with Booth. "You see, my friend, we must wait."

"Yes," Booth agreed, "I leave it all with you."

On the morning of the seventeenth, another man waited, too. Troops still had not called on Dr. Mudd to pursue his tip — because they still did not know about it! It wasn't until the next afternoon that George Mudd rode into Bryantown. He made a vague report to Lieutenant Dana: Two suspicious strangers visited his cousin's farm seeking medical attention. Then, in another unbelievable stroke of good luck for Booth and Herold, Dana ignored the news as old and unimportant. He thanked George Mudd and sent him on his way. He did not send troops to Mudd's farm to investigate. Distracted by other leads, many of them dead ends, Lieutenant Dana ignored the one tip that placed Lincoln's assassin within his reach.

When soldiers had not come by his farm by that evening, Dr. Mudd relaxed. Perhaps, at this point, they would not come at all. With the assassin's trail in Maryland growing cold, the soldiers would soon leave and shift the action to other places far from Bryantown and his farm.

Thomas Jones had experienced enough excitement for one day. He agreed to return to the thicket to feed Booth and Herold the next morning, but he refused to bring horse feed again. It was difficult to carry enough feed for the horses, and Jones feared a passing cavalry patrol would hear their horses, which were hungry, restless, and noisy. The horses had served them well, and Herold loved animals, but they all agreed that the horses must be disposed of. The horses' reward for faithful service was death. Herold led them to a quicksand pit about a mile away, shot them, and then sank their bodies.

Herold returned to the thicket and sat on the ground beside Booth. Never during their escape were they more vulnerable and alone. If the Union cavalry found them now, they would not be able to make a run for it. Exhausted and injured, Booth could not hope to outrun a mounted pursuit. And if Thomas Jones abandoned them, how would they find a way to cross the river? Later, in the safety of the night, Booth and Herold rolled out their woolen blankets and spent another night on the ground.

CHAPTER VIII

In Washington, the occupants of Mary Surratt's boardinghouse prepared for bed, too. That evening the authorities paid another visit to put pressure on Mary and her daughter, Anna. The manhunters were desperate. Three days after the assassination, John Wilkes Booth was still on the run. Seward's attacker was a mystery man — Stanton did not even know the assailant's name. John Surratt was suspected in the Seward attack, but there was no proof.

Major W. H. Smith went to Surratt's boardinghouse to arrest the residents and search the house. Smith and his men questioned Mary, Anna, and other residents, then summoned a carriage to transport the women to headquarters.

Just then, a man walking down H Street wandered up the front steps of the house, knocked on the front door, and rang the bell. It was soldiers and not Mrs. Surratt who opened the door to him. He stood before them, a large, powerful-looking man, carrying a pickax. He was dressed in a gray coat, black pants, and a fine pair of boots. As soon as the man stepped inside and into the hall, a soldier shut the door behind him. The man immediately sensed that something was wrong. He said he was there to see Mrs. Surratt. The officer told him he was in the right place and began to question him. The officer wanted to know the man's occupation, why he was there so late at night, how old he was, and where he lived.

The man claimed that he was there to find out what time he should start work digging a gutter for Mrs. Surratt in the morning. He said she had offered him the job when she had seen him working in the neighborhood.

The soldier asked Mrs. Surratt to confirm the man's story. She stood three steps from Lewis Powell as the soldier asked, "Do you know this man? And did you hire him to come and dig a gutter for you?" Her eyes locked on the man's face in recognition. He was Lewis Powell, Seward's would-be assassin. Powell's remarkable face was unforgettable, and he had been to her home at least twice before.

Mary raised her right hand as if swearing an oath. "Before God, sir, I do not know this man; and I have never seen him and did not hire him to dig a gutter for me."

Powell looked at Mary in silence. Lewis Powell had been caught in a lie. Now he was trapped in this house full of soldiers. In moments, they would surely try to seize and

NATIONAL POLICE GAZETTE.

GEORGE W. MATSELL & CO.

NEW YORK: FOR THE WEEK ENDING APRIL 29, 1865. VOL. XX. NO. 1026.—[PRICE TEN CENTS.

Booth Escaping from the Theatre after the Assassination of the President.

Conveying the President from the Theatre to the House of Mr. Peterson.

Identification of Payne by the Negro Servant as the Assassin of Sec. Seward.

Arrest of Payne at the House of Surratt.

Tarring and Feathering at Swampscott, Mass., of a Justifier of the Assassin.

Arrest of G. A. Atzerot, one of the Conspirators against the Life of Pres. Lincoln.

arrest him. Powell was armed only with a pickax, but his incredible strength could turn that tool into a formidable weapon. If Powell chose to fight, he could certainly do great harm to a few of the soldiers before being captured or before being shot in the confusion. Powell glared at the soldiers. He could swing that ax quicker than they could draw their pistols. It was his move. Then, surprisingly, meekly, without protest, he surrendered without a fight.

If Lewis Powell had not wandered into the government's hands this night, he might have escaped Washington and vanished from history. Instead, the government celebrated his capture as the first major break in the manhunt. Within hours, Seward's servant identified Powell as the knife-wielding maniac.

The soldiers arrested Powell, Mary Surratt, her daughter, Anna, Lewis Weichmann, and the rest of the boarders. They searched the house and found evidence: photographs of Confederate generals, one of Confederate President Jefferson Davis, some ammunition, and a photo of John Wilkes Booth, hidden behind a picture frame.

At headquarters, the interrogator, Colonel Wells, wanted to know what had brought Mary's son and John Wilkes Booth together, about her son's relationship with the other possible conspirators, and what her connection was to the newly arrested Lewis Powell. Mary Surratt proved to be cool and collected under questioning. She revealed nothing to help the authorities to find Booth. She only admitted facts she was sure her questioners knew from other sources, especially her connection to Booth. She lied when she claimed she met Powell for the first time that evening as he arrived at her house while the soldiers were there. She admitted to knowing George Atzerodt, something the government already knew. Atzerodt was already connected to Booth from the evidence recovered in the search of the German's room at the Kirkwood House. Mary Surratt did not tell Colonel Wells about Booth's April 14 visit to her, the binoculars, her carriage ride to Surrattsville, nor her instructions about the "shooting irons."

The questioning over for now, Wells refused to let Mary return home. He sent her to the Old Capitol Prison, where she would join the many other suspects and witnesses arrested after the president's murder. Though she did not suspect it that night, Mary Surratt would never see her boardinghouse again.

With the arrests of Sam Arnold, Michael O'Laughlen, and Edman Spangler, Monday, April 17 closed as the most successful day in the three-day-old manhunt. Arnold, a thirty-one-year-old Confederate army veteran and former schoolmate of Booth's, was arrested based on a tip. He confessed that he participated in Booth's earlier scheme to kidnap the president, but he denied involvement in, or knowledge of, the assassination plot.

Michael O'Laughlen, a twenty-eight-year-old childhood friend of Booth's, another former Confederate soldier and participant in the kidnapping plot, was also arrested on the seventeenth.

Edman Spangler, the thirty-nine-year-old stagehand from Ford's Theatre, was also arrested. His crime was briefly holding the reins of Booth's horse in the alley behind Ford's Theatre. Poor Spangler had nothing to do with the assassination or the earlier kidnapping plot. His long association with Booth, holding the mare's reins, and the claim by another theater employee that Spangler did not tell pursuers which way Booth went down the alley earned Edman a cell in the Old Capitol Prison for the remainder of the manhunt.

Many other people in the theater were rounded up, including the Fords. Stanton suspected the participation in the plot by other theater employees: How else could Booth have escaped so smoothly and easily? The theater itself was "arrested," ordered closed, and was eventually confiscated from the Fords.

The dragnet of the manhunters eventually rounded up more than one hundred suspects. The arrests filled the headlines, but Booth, the most famous and recognizable man in America, remained free.

Edwin Stanton needed help. He would be unable to continue to devote all of his time and brainpower to the manhunt. He had a war to finish. Just because Lee had surrendered his army did not mean the war was over for Stanton. Other Confederate armies remained in the field in some Southern states. Some generals had not yet surrendered. Confederate President Jefferson Davis was on the run, the subject of his own massive manhunt. Stanton had the War Department and Union army to run and the reconstruction of the South to plan. He had to investigate the assassination, capture the conspirators, and organize a military tribunal to try them. It was more than one mind, even Stanton's, could manage. He had to delegate authority to a small circle of trusted manhunters, including Lieutenant Lafayette Baker, newly arrived from New York.

CHAPTER IX

When John Wilkes Booth planned the assassination and his escape, he did not prepare for an extended campout under the stars. He focused on the need for speed, not camping in the forests of Maryland, cowering like a wounded animal, fearful that every noise meant the hunters were about to seize him.

Traveling light had served him well in the first part of his escape, but left him unprepared for this unanticipated phase of his journey. He left Washington wearing the equivalent of a modern-day business suit, unsuitable for camping out. Without a change of clothing, his garments quickly became dirty, ruining a key element of Booth's trademark, winning style — his beautifully dressed, well-groomed appearance. He and Herold could not bathe or wash clothes and, unshaven, they looked and smelled worse each day. They looked like the fugitives they were. Their looks might even jeopardize their ability to receive a proper reception at the fine Virginia households they planned to call on across the river.

On the morning of Tuesday, April 18, Jones paid his third call on the fugitives. With each visit, he risked capture, arrest, or worse. Soldiers had visited his farm several times and searched his house once. Jones handed over food and newspapers, then quickly left Booth and Herold alone again. Booth's curiosity about the country's reaction to the events of the last four days was limitless. Eager for the papers Jones had brought him, what he read stunned him.

Whatever papers Booth read, they all condemned him for his heinous act. Even worse, Booth saw the beginning of a change in how Abraham Lincoln was viewed by America. Lincoln was transformed from a controversial and often unpopular war leader into a martyr and hero. Stories reported in the papers condemned Booth by name in the most unforgiving, vicious language. The accounts of the Seward attack stunned Booth. Had Powell gone insane? Yes, Seward had been a target, but the viciousness of the assault shocked and revolted Booth. Why had Powell attacked the sons? The daughter? The nurse?

Booth searched the papers for the article he had written the day of the assassination. He had entrusted the letter to an actor friend, who was to deliver it to the *National Intelligencer* for publication. Incredibly, not one newspaper published or even mentioned his letter. But he was wrong to think the newspapers or government was suppressing his letter: His friend, terrified of being connected to the assassin, never delivered the letter to the newspaper. He burned it.

Booth wanted to explain why he killed Lincoln. He opened his small date book. In hurried, cramped writing, he began his letter to history. He explained some of the reasons he had assassinated Lincoln: He longed for the South as it was and deplored the Union. He gave details about how he had committed the act.

Booth was not the only conspirator shocked at what he read in the papers. In Elmira, New York, John Surratt read accounts that mistakenly identified him as Seward's attacker! Though John Surratt had been a conspirator in the kidnapping plot, he was not even in Washington on the evening of the assassination.

Tuesday, April 18, acting on what was now a stale tip, a cavalry officer decided to follow up on the information about the mysterious strangers who stopped by Mudd's farm on assassination night. The soldier sent for George Mudd but, as a witness, George Mudd was useless. He only knew what his cousin Samuel Mudd had told him. The manhunters decided to pursue the lead to its source. The men mounted up, heading for Samuel Mudd's farm, taking George Mudd with them.

When they arrived at the farm, the soldiers questioned first Mrs. Mudd, then Dr. Mudd. Samuel Mudd had plenty of time to concoct his story. If he behaved naturally and did nothing to arouse suspicion, all would be well. Mudd told the soldiers the bare bones of what had happened: Two strangers on horseback arrived near daybreak, one had a broken leg, and he set the bone. The injured man rested in the parlor. The strangers did not stay long. He gave vague and general descriptions of the two men. One soldier asked if Mudd knew the men. No, the doctor replied, they were complete strangers to him. Mudd then attempted to send the manhunters on a wild goose chase, claiming the strangers asked for directions to a farm to the west. His story was full of lies and half-truths. He had passed the point of no return: He had given aid and comfort to Abraham Lincoln's killers and now he lied about it to protect them.

The soldiers searched the barn and other buildings on the farm but found nothing. After about an hour, the patrol left. If Mudd thought he had cleared himself, he was wrong. The lieutenant had decided Mudd was guilty of *something* and he would arrest him sooner or later.

In Washington, on the morning of April 19, the most solemn day in the history of the nation began with the president's funeral. On Pennsylvania Avenue, thousands of people jostled for a place from which they would see the funeral procession pass as it left the White House. Six magnificent white horses drawing a carriage carrying Abraham Lincoln's coffin made their way up the avenue. Every building lining the avenue wept with black crepe. The procession rolled slowly, the beat of the march measured by drums wrapped in crepe. Lincoln's funeral procession was the saddest, most profoundly moving spectacle ever staged in the history of the United States. Thousands of citizens would wait for hours to view Lincoln's open casket under the great dome inside the Capitol. When the funeral was over, the president's body would be placed aboard a special train that could carry him home to Springfield.

While tens of thousands of mourners viewed Lincoln's remains, detectives prepared to raid the Philadelphia home of the assassin's sister, Asia Booth Clarke. They searched for and confiscated anything and everything connected to John Wilkes Booth, including documents unconnected to the assassination.

In the early morning hours of April 20, in Maryland, two teams of detectives were planning a raid that would take George Atzerodt. He had spent the last four nights at his cousin's place, not moved to flee by the great risk of capture he faced. Atzerodt should have known the detectives would have searched his room at the Kirkwood and discovered his connection to Booth. He had foolishly aroused suspicion when he made unusual comments about the assassination over dinner in the presence of guests. One of the guests reported his statement to a local Union informant, who passed the tip along to soldiers who were now at the door at Hartmann Richter's place to pick up Atzerodt.

When Richter answered the soldiers' knock, the soldiers asked whether Atzerodt was there. When Richter said he had been there but had left, a soldier said he would search

WE LOVED HIM IN LIFE

WE MOURN HIM IN DEATH.

Born Feb. 12, 1809.
Died April 15, 1865.

People expressed their grief by wearing white silk ribbons printed in black.

The Nation Mourns a Martyred Father.

Small, colorful paper flags were popular symbols of mourning for the slain president.

the house anyway. Richter then admitted that Atzerodt was upstairs. The manhunters found Atzerodt in bed. He surrendered without a fight, not even asking why he was being taken.

Atzerodt confessed all. The man questioning him did not even have to apply pressure. Atzerodt told him many details about the plot to kill Lincoln, the kidnapping plot, and the conspirators' final meeting on April 14. He implicated Mary Surratt and Dr. Mudd. Now the War Department had its hands on two of the four men — Powell and Atzerodt — who were in the inner circle of the conspiracy.

Following Atzerodt's arrest, Stanton issued a new proclamation: A reward was posted offering $100,000 — an enormous sum — for Lincoln's killers. The poster included photos of Booth, Herold, and John Surratt, the most wanted men in the country.

CHAPTER X

On Thursday, April 20, Thomas Jones witnessed the cavalry riding out of town on the news that the assassins had been spotted in another county. Jones concealed his excitement as the soldiers rode away. Once safely out of view of the village, he wasted no time in getting back to the thicket. He emitted the three-note whistle. Herold appeared and led Jones to Booth. This late-night visit from Jones could only mean one thing. It was now or never!

They had waited in the pine thicket for four nights. This was the night they would attempt to cross the Potomac River to sanctuary in Virginia on the other side. The three made their way down a series of hidden paths and public roads, Booth riding, the others on foot. Their first destination was Jones's farm. Jones slipped into the house and, without a word, scooped from the supper table enough food for two men and carried it out of the house.

The fugitives ate, then immediately headed for the river,

SURRAT.   BOOTH.   HAROLD.

War Department, Washington, April 20, 1865,

 # $100,000 REWARD!

THE MURDERER

Of our late beloved President, Abraham Lincoln,

IS STILL AT LARGE.

$50,000 REWARD

Will be paid by this Department for his apprehension, in addition to any reward offered by Municipal Authorities or State Executives.

$25,000 REWARD

Will be paid for the apprehension of JOHN H. SURRATT, one of Booth's Accomplices.

$25,000 REWARD

Will be paid for the apprehension of David C. Harold, another of Booth's accomplices.

LIBERAL REWARDS will be paid for any information that shall conduce to the arrest of either of the above-named criminals, or their accomplices.

All persons harboring or secreting the said persons, or either of them, or aiding or assisting their concealment or escape, will be treated as accomplices in the murder of the President, and the attempted assassination of the Secretary of State, and shall be subject to trial

Let the stain of innocent bloo[...]

All good citizens are exhorte[...]
charged with this solemn duty, an[...]

DESCRIPTIONS.—BOOTH [...]
wears a heavy black moustache.

JOHN H. SURRAT is about [...]
weigh 145 or 150 pounds. Com[...]
quality. Shoulders square; chee[...]
low and square, but broad. Part[...]

DAVID C. HAROLD is five [...]
hand short and fleshy, feet small, instep high, round bodied, naturally quick and active, slightly closes his eyes when looking at a person.

NOTICE.—In addition to the above, State and other authorities have offered rewards amounting to almost one hundred thousand dollars, making an aggregate of about **TWO HUNDRED THOUSAND DOLLARS.**

Six days after the assassination, John Wilkes Booth and his accomplices were still on the loose. Secretary of War Edwin M. Stanton offered a reward of $100,000 for their capture and threatened death to anyone who aided the fugitives.

about a mile away. They would use a fishing boat Jones had arranged for his servant to leave by the river.

Jones waded into the shallows and brought in the boat. He and Herold helped Booth struggle into the craft, laying the weapons and crutches on the hull of the boat. They handed him an oar to steer with. Herold settled in the bow seat to row. Jones crouched down, took a candle from his coat pocket, and told Booth to take out his compass. Jones held the dripping candle over the protective glass cover that shielded the dancing compass needle, showing Booth the course to steer. Jones handed Booth the candle, cautioning him to hide its faint glow during the crossing, lest they be spotted by passing patrol boats. Then Jones gave Booth the name of a contact on the other side.

As Jones grabbed the stern of the boat and shoved it off, a grateful Booth thrust a fistful of Union greenbacks at Jones. Jones refused the gesture, saying that he had not helped him for money. Under protest, he agreed to accept just eighteen dollars, the price he had paid for the boat.

Jones shoved them off; Herold gripped the oars and rowed toward the Virginia shore, two miles away. The river was dark as ink, and the boat soon vanished against the glass-smooth black surface of the strong current under a moonless night.

Thomas Jones never saw Booth, Herold, or his boat again. He made his way back to his farm along deserted roads. One clever man had just outwitted the manhunters. While a frustrated nation sought vengeance, Jones had sheltered and nourished the most hated man in America. They should be landing in Virginia about now, thought Jones. But while Jones slept peacefully, John Wilkes Booth and David Herold were rowing in the wrong direction!

Also on April 20, Dr. Mudd was questioned again by the cavalry. Mudd feared the authorities would discover some of his secrets very soon. He thought it might go better for him if he volunteered at least part of the truth. He told Lieutenant Lovett that the man with the broken leg was armed, that he wore a false beard. Most interesting of all, he revealed to one of the manhunters that he knew John Wilkes Booth. He had met him last fall.

In Bryantown, Colonel Wells found it odd that Mudd had failed to recognize a man he had met before, and not just briefly — especially when that man was so famous. After all, Mudd and Booth had met on several occasions, in broad daylight, and Booth had slept at Mudd's farm in the past.

After hours of questioning, Colonel Wells showed Mudd another photograph of Lincoln's killer and asked him whether he recognized the man in the picture as the stranger. On second thought, Mudd admitted, he realized it just now. The stranger was John Wilkes Booth! Unintentionally or unknowingly, Mudd claimed, he had helped him escape. Exhausted by the questioning, after agreeing to return to Bryantown the next day to sign a statement, Mudd rode home.

In a few hours, Booth and Herold would reach Virginia, far from the reach of Colonel Wells, his detectives, and Lieutenant Dana and the cavalry. Mudd's lies delayed the cavalry's departure long enough to allow the fugitives to escape Maryland.

Thomas Jones would eventually be questioned by Union detectives. They suspected that a man of his reputation must know something of Booth's escape. They arrested him and eventually imprisoned him. But with no eyewitnesses who could place him with Booth, and him not volunteering anything, he was eventually released, as was Captain Cox. Decades later, when his confession could no longer hurt Booth, Thomas Jones did tell his story to a journalist who recorded it for history.

Herold dipped the blades of the oars deep and pulled hard. After spending so much time in the pine thicket — a lost week — it felt good to be on the move again. Booth checked the compass bearings. They were supposed to be rowing from Maryland west across the Potomac to Virginia, then south. But the needle on the compass indicated they were headed north. Was the compass broken? No, the compass was true. Herold was a good enough navigator during the daylight, but not under cloak of darkness, and not haunted by the fear of capture. He had been rowing for far too long: They should be in Virginia by now. His palms and fingers were sore, and his burning arm and leg muscles made it clear that they had already traveled too far. They had to land soon. Herold spotted a familiar-looking landmark: Blossom Point, at the mouth of a creek that ran north. The good news was that he knew the area and had friends there who would help them. The bad news was that they were back in Maryland. And they were farther north than they had been the night before. That left them vulnerable once more to Union patrols that were pursuing them.

They landed the boat at the mouth of a creek in Maryland early in the morning, Friday, April 21. Booth and Herold gathered their weapons and blankets and headed on foot to the nearby house of a friend of Herold's, where they were fed, and given information. Union troops and detectives were swarming the countryside, motivated in part by the enormous reward being offered by the War Department. The geography of the place they landed made it impossible for them to escape except by crossing the Potomac. Herold and Booth would have to hide in the low-lying wetlands and wait to cross. At this critical moment, when they needed to escape Maryland as quickly as possible, they did something unexplainable — they did nothing! They did not retrieve the boat and row across the river. They sat in the dark and did nothing. They would have to spend another day hiding in Maryland until the following evening when darkness came.

While Booth and Herold tarried, the government pursued them with new energy. The evidence gathered at Mudd's farm, plus alleged sightings of the fugitives southwest of his farm, suggested that the assassins were making for Virginia. They knew Booth was lame, on crutches. They knew he had shaven off his mustache. Horse-mounted couriers and telegraph wires were alive all day with instructions to troops to enlist the help of fishermen and others on the river to capture the fugitives.

CHAPTER XI

On the night of April 22, after another night's delay, John Wilkes Booth and David Herold finally climbed aboard the boat and rowed out into the Potomac toward Virginia. This time, they steered the correct course and, after several hours, spotted their destination — the mouth of a creek on the Virginia side of the Potomac. They landed and disembarked. At last, on April 23, nine days after the assassination, John Wilkes Booth and David Herold set foot on Virginia soil.

Their contact, a former Confederate agent, Mrs. Quesenberry, had a place about half an hour away on foot. Booth's injured leg made the brief walk impossible for him, so Herold went alone to find the woman.

Elizabeth Quesenberry, an ex-Confederate spy, was cautious when Herold approached her. Experience during the war had taught her to be suspicious of strangers, especially those who looked like Herold. Herold revealed that Thomas

Jones had sent him to her, which put her mind at ease. Herold revealed the nature of his request for help.

He was traveling with an injured companion. They needed horses to make their way south. Suspecting or already knowing who the two strangers were, Mrs. Quesenberry decided that this was too big a job to handle by herself. With the help of other loyal operatives, she arranged for horses. She would get the two moving south as quickly as possible. Speed was now of the essence.

Mrs. Quesenberry arranged for horses and food, which Herold brought to the waiting Booth. After eating, they saddled up. Dr. Richard Stuart's house was the next stop on their journey. To their dismay, the doctor refused to help them. Herold pleaded their case, mentioning their Confederate credentials and the recommendation from Dr. Mudd. Stuart, unconvinced and suspicious of the elaborate and ridiculous cover story Herold spun for him, reluctantly offered to feed them. After eating, they would have to be on their way.

Dr. Stuart was a great disappointment, failing to display the Southern hospitality and honor that Booth had come to expect. Booth and Herold sat down to dinner with Stuart and his family. How out of place these dirty, tired travelers must have seemed at the Stuarts' fine table. But Booth's filthy clothes, unshaven face, and pungent body could not conceal his obvious good breeding. His excellent manners, educated voice, and physical poise marked him as a gentleman.

By now, Dr. Stuart knew exactly who his visitors were. They were dirty, desperate, and on the run. And one had a broken leg. They fit the profile of the men now known to the whole country as Lincoln's assassins. After dinner, Stuart practically ordered Booth and Herold to leave his home, which they did without protest.

Later Booth would write a letter to Dr. Stuart, chiding him for his lack of Southern hospitality and honor. As an insult, Booth enclosed a small sum of money as a payment for the meal they had eaten, but not enjoyed, at Stuart's.

Denied a bed and hospitality for the night, Booth and Herold continued to search for transportation at the house of one of Stuart's neighbors, a man of color named Lucas. Lucas, too, was reluctant to help the strangers. Under protest, he finally agreed to rent them a team of horses and a wagon, with his son Charlie acting as driver for the trip south. It took threats of violence by Booth to persuade Lucas to allow the fugitives to stay the night at his cabin. In the morning, Booth paid twenty dollars for the use of the wagon, the team, and driver.

When they arrived at their destination, Port Conway, young Charlie Lucas stopped the wagon in front of the home of William Rollins, a farmer and fisherman. There Booth and Herold quenched their thirst and sought a ride south, across the Rappahannock River to Port Royal, then on to a nearby railroad station.

The tide was rising, and the fisherman was eager to prepare for the day's catch. He agreed to ferry Booth and Herold across the river as soon as he set his fishing nets. At that moment, three mounted figures appeared on the hill just above Port Conway. They were soldiers! And the wagon driven by Charlie Lucas, parked in front of William Rollins's house, caught their attention. The men spurred their horses and descended into town.

Booth and Herold tensed for action. An encounter with soldiers was inevitable. Herold walked toward the riders as they approached, creating distance between them and Booth. The jackets the soldiers wore were not the blue of Union soldiers. A few casual questions and Herold determined they were Confederates! These were soldiers likely to be sympathetic to their plight. Herold gave the soldiers false names and claimed he and Booth were on their way to join up with the Confederates themselves. He pretended he was an enthusiastic militant Confederate eager to continue to fight the war, wherever it was. One of the soldiers, Willie Jett, reacted skeptically to Herold's story. He asked a simple question: "Who are you?"

Herold replied, his voice trembling, "We are the assassinators of the president! . . . Yonder is J. Wilkes Booth, the man who killed the president." Jett told the other two soldiers, Ruggles and Bainbridge, the exciting news he had just learned.

When Rollins returned from setting his nets, he asked Booth if he was ready to be ferried across the river now. The soldiers huddled with the fugitives and hatched a plan. They would accompany the assassins in the ferryboat and help them on the other side. To the man who piloted the men across the river, the strangers were unremarkable, just another band of bedraggled rebels heading home after losing the war. The successful crossing represented a high point of this phase of the escape. After many disappointments, they had crossed safely south and found loyal Confederate comrades. Overcome with emotion, Booth shouted out, "I'm safe in glorious old Virginia, thank God!"

Willie Jett, Ruggles, Bainbridge, and the fugitives made their way to Locust Hill, a farm owned by Richard H. Garrett, seeking shelter for the night. Willie introduced himself and presented Booth: "Here is a wounded Confederate soldier that we want you to take care of for a day or so. Will you do it?"

Garrett thought of his sons, who had returned from the war safely just a few days ago. He would return that blessing with a kindness. He agreed to take them in.

The soldiers took Herold with them on a ride into a nearby town while Booth spent the night of April 24 at Garrett's farm. Booth spun a believable tale for the Garretts.

He had been wounded in battle and was now being chased by the Union cavalry.

Until now, most of the investigation and manhunt were focused on southern Maryland. That was about to change. Lafayette Baker, the notorious detective and War Department agent — and a favorite of Stanton's — had been in Washington since April 16. Since his arrival, his deceitful, egotistical, and self-promoting ways had rubbed a number of the manhunters the wrong way. He even tried to steal other detectives' leads. He was snooping around the telegraph office when the message came in: Two men had been seen crossing the Potomac. This report required action! Lafayette Baker seized the telegram, rushed back to his headquarters, and alerted his cousin Luther Byron Baker to the news of the sighting. Lafayette said, "I think Booth has crossed the river and I want you to go right out."

Yes, two men had been seen crossing the river on April 16. But they were not Booth and Herold.

A telegraphed order to the commander of the Sixteenth New York Cavalry ordered a commissioned officer, Lieutenant Edward P. Doherty, to report to Luther Byron Baker. Baker handed him freshly printed photographs of three men. Doherty did not recognize two of them, but the third man was John Wilkes Booth. He was going after Lincoln's assassin!

While Colonel Baker stayed behind in Washington to monitor telegraph traffic and protect his interest in the

Colonel Lafayette C. Baker and aides are depicted taking charge of the search for Booth. Although Baker had the trust of the secretary of war, he was a shady character who thwarted others hunting for Booth, claimed more credit than he deserved, and sought a large share of the reward money.

reward money, Edward Doherty, Luther Baker, and Everton Conger made their way across the water by steamboat, landing in Virginia. From there, the troops traveled south over land on horseback. If they kept moving, the soldiers of the Sixteenth New York would reach the same spot where the fugitives had crossed the Rappahannock by tomorrow afternoon, April 25.

That evening, John Wilkes Booth enjoyed a leisurely supper with the Garretts. He relished the company and the genuine hospitality, so different from Dr. Stuart's impolite, hostile reception. Herold rode into the nearby town of Bowling Green with the Confederates to purchase, of all things, a new pair of shoes. He would spend the night with them and rejoin Booth tomorrow, April 25, at Garrett's farm. Booth would sleep in a real bed tonight. It had been days since he had slept in a proper bed, and this was the first night since the assassination that Booth and Herold spent apart.

Nearby, the cavalry divided their forces. One column was commanded by Everton Conger, one by Edward Doherty. They searched farmhouses and barns, questioned the occupants, making their way south to Port Conway. Booth's head start over the manhunters began to shrink. It had taken Booth ten days to travel from Washington to the Port Conway ferry. It would take the cavalry, alerted by telegraph and traveling by steamboat, just one day to travel that distance.

On Monday, April 24, Dr. Samuel A. Mudd saw soldiers, too. They had come to his farm to arrest him and take him to the Old Capitol Prison. Confined and isolated, Mudd would wait to learn what price he would have to pay for his part in hiding Lincoln's assassins.

The morning of April 25, Booth slept in. He talked and played with the Garrett children. He showed them his pocket compass, delighting them by making the needle dance when he held the point of his pocketknife above it. Early in the afternoon, the Garretts and Booth sat at the dinner table. Young John Garrett, back from an errand at a neighboring farm, reported that the U.S. government was offering a $140,000 reward for Abraham Lincoln's assassin. The family discussed the assassination with Booth, speculating on why the murderer did it. The actor, still masquerading as a Confederate soldier, commented on his own crime and analyzed for the Garretts the motives of Lincoln's killer!

Booth needed rest and would happily have spent a month with the Garretts recovering from his injury and regaining his strength. But it was time to move on. He asked for a map of Virginia. He said he would make his way to the town of Orange Court House, where he hoped to get a horse. He would ride south to join a Confederate army still in the field.

Booth should have left hours ago. He was too far north, within striking distance of Union troops.

Booth came out onto the porch. He became agitated when he saw riders moving past the farm's front gate. To his obvious relief, the men just rode by. The danger was over for the moment. But Richard Garrett was alarmed by Booth's reaction to the riders. Five minutes later, a lone man walked up the road to the farm. Booth asked eleven-year-old Richard Jr. to run and fetch his pistols and gun belt from his room upstairs. The Garretts expected a gun battle to break out in their yard at any moment. But Booth did not draw his pistols. It was David Herold, returning from his overnight stay a few miles south.

To David Herold's dismay, Booth intended to spend another night at the farm. He would ask the Garretts for another night of hospitality for him and for Herold. With his father temporarily away from the farm on business, it fell to son John to decide whether to take in not one but two men. To their surprise, John Garrett refused to take them in for the night. Booth's panic at the sight of the riders was a tip-off: Something was not right. John Garrett was suspicious of Booth now.

The Sixteenth New York Cavalry rode into Port Conway on Tuesday, April 25, late in the afternoon. Luther Baker spotted William Rollins, the man who had offered to ferry Booth, Herold, Jett, Ruggles, and Bainbridge to Port Royal. From questioning Rollins, Baker discovered that a man with a broken leg had crossed the river the day before, around noon. It must be Booth! That meant the fugitives were only about a day's ride ahead of them. Baker learned something else that interested him: Booth was now in the company of three Confederate soldiers. That could add to the danger of the mission to capture Booth. Rollins then identified photographs of Herold and Booth. Rollins and his wife also identified the three rebel soldiers: Willie Jett, Ruggles, and Bainbridge. In a stroke of luck, they also had an idea where Willie Jett might be headed: Jett had been courting a young lady whose father kept a hotel in the nearby town of Bowling Green. The soldiers' next destination was clear: Cross the Rappahannock, then on to look for Jett.

It was 4:00 P.M. on Tuesday, April 25. John Garrett worried about what to do with his now unwanted guests. Soon two horsemen, riding quickly from the direction of Port Royal, galloped toward the house at high speed. Booth and Herold left the front porch to meet them. Ruggles and Bainbridge hurried to bring the news — the Union cavalry was coming! The Confederates had seen the patrol crossing the Rappahannock on the ferry. Worse news, the patrol had seen the Confederates watching them from the ridge overlooking the ferry.

Bainbridge and Ruggles turned their horses around and galloped away, heading away from where they had seen the patrol. Booth and Herold looked at each other and, without exchanging a word, ran for the woods behind Garrett's barn and waited. No cavalry arrived.

If Booth's agitation about the riders worried Garrett, his flight into the woods with Herold frightened him even more. John Garrett complained forcefully, asking them to leave the house. While he argued with them, a thunderous sound shook the earth. "There goes the cavalry now!" Garrett exclaimed. It was Union soldiers but, incredibly, they rode right past the front gate and raced on toward Bowling Green in pursuit of Willie Jett! John Garrett, certain Herold knew the patrol's purpose, asked them again to leave at once.

Once again, Booth and Herold needed transportation. Where could they find horses or hire a team and a wagon? Garrett agreed to help them, taking them where they wanted to go himself if necessary. To his dismay, Booth and Herold said they did not want to leave until morning!

The mood at the dinner table this night differed from the friendly atmosphere the night before. The reluctant hosts talked no more of the Lincoln assassination. After supper, the fugitives again discussed where they might find transportation, probably horses. The Civil War had consumed most of the good horses in the South; they were scarce and valuable. John Garrett grew increasingly suspicious of the strangers: Did they intend to steal horses from the Garretts?

Booth and Herold sat on the front porch, watching the

evening sky's last clouds and colors fade to black. The scent of the spring night filled their nostrils until the sweetly burning smoke rising from Booth's pipe flavored the air. The reluctant Garretts had nourished and sustained Booth for another day. Tomorrow morning, Wednesday, April 26, he would continue his journey south. It would be the twelfth day.

But first, they would rest another night. They planned to spend the night in the bed Garrett had offered Booth the night before. John Garrett stunned the two by barking out that they could not sleep in the house. Could they sleep under the house, then? Impossible, said Garrett, the dogs sleep there and would bite them. Herold put the matter to rest, announcing they would sleep in the tobacco barn, then. John Garrett still did not know the identity of the man he was throwing out of his house. He was pretty sure the two were in some kind of trouble, but it was unlikely he knew it was Lincoln's killer who was a guest at his family's dinner table.

Booth and Herold headed toward the tobacco barn, which stood a hundred feet or so from the main house. It was forty-eight feet by fifty feet, with a slanted roof and wide, open slats in the walls. By 9:00 P.M., Booth and Herold had unrolled their blankets and settled in for the night. They were unaware that the Garretts, already guilty of inhospitality, were conspiring to commit a worse offense: treachery. Lincoln's assassin had just walked into a trap.

The Garretts swung the barn door shut behind the fugitives. Neither Booth nor Herold paid attention to the black iron lock on the door as they passed through the doorway. John Garrett was sure the men were scheming to steal their horses in the middle of the night. What better way to prevent that than by locking the strangers in the tobacco shed until morning? His brother William tiptoed to the front door and, as quietly as he could, inserted the key into the lock. The fugitives did not hear the sliding bolt, did not know they were prisoners. Then brothers John and William Garrett grabbed blankets and a pistol and spent the night in the corn house, watching the tobacco barn and waiting, listening for suspicious sounds in the night.

At 11:00 P.M., the cavalry patrol approached Bowling Green. They surrounded the Star Hotel, expecting to find Willie Jett inside. The proprietor of the house led the soldiers to a second-story bedroom. Prepared for anything, the officer and detectives rushed in and discovered Willie. They seized him, hustled him downstairs roughly, and confined him in the parlor. Doherty, Baker, and Conger worked on Jett, trying to frighten him. Conger asked, "Where are the two men who came with you across the river at Port Royal?" Jett betrayed John Wilkes Booth: "I know who you want and I will tell you where they can be found." He revealed the fugitives were at Richard Garrett's farmhouse and agreed to show the soldiers where they were. Without Jett's help, it might be difficult, almost impossible, to locate the Garrett farm in the middle of the night.

It was day twelve. At about 12:30 A.M., the Sixteenth New York Cavalry headed for Garrett's farm and, they hoped, the capture of Lincoln's assassin.

Once at the front gate of the Garrett farm, a charge was ordered. The Sixteenth New York Cavalry raced up the dirt road toward the farmhouse.

The Garretts' dogs heard the noise first: the sound of metal touching metal, of one hundred hooves sending vibrations through the earth. On watch, John and William Garrett heard it, too. The barking of the dogs and clanking metal sounds finally woke Booth. Recognizing the unique music of cavalry on the move, the assassin knew he had only a minute or two to react before it was too late.

The cavalry is here, Booth hissed as he woke Herold. They snatched up their weapons and rushed to the front of the barn, where they discovered the door was locked! The Garretts had imprisoned them! Booth tried to pry the lock from its mountings. They had to flee immediately, before the Union troops could surround them. They scampered to the back wall of the barn and tried to kick out a board so they could crawl out. With Booth's injured leg, even working together, he and Herold could not dislodge a board so they could escape to the woods.

The Union column raced up the road and surrounded

the farmhouse. Edward Doherty, Luther Baker, and Everton Conger dropped from their saddles, leaped up onto the porch, and pounded on the door. Richard Garrett climbed from his bed and walked downstairs in his nightclothes.

In the tobacco barn, David Herold panicked. "You had better give up," he urged.

No, no, the actor insisted, "I will suffer death first."

Conger demanded of Richard Garrett, "Where are the two men who stopped here at your house?" Garrett turned out to be very reluctant to reveal Booth and Herold's whereabouts. Even the threat of hanging did not move Richard Garrett to reveal where the prey were hiding. Then Doherty seized John Garrett and put a revolver to his head, ordering him to tell where the assassins were.

"In the barn," he slowly revealed, "they are in the tobacco barn." The soldiers rushed to surround the barn. Baker ordered John Garrett to enter the barn and take the weapons from the fugitives. John had seen Booth's weapons and knew he would not hesitate to take revenge for his family's inhospitality and betrayal. No, he would not be the assassin's last victim. Baker explained that the mission was not optional. If he did not go to the barn, Baker would burn all of the Garrett property. He would "end this affair with a bonfire and shooting match."

Baker unlocked the barn door, opened it a little, with Booth invisible just a few yards away. He clutched his pistols tightly but held his fire. Baker seized John Garrett and half-guided, half-pushed him through the door and closed it behind him.

John Garrett urged Booth, still hidden in the dark, to give himself up. Like a ghostly vision, John Wilkes Booth's pale, haunting face emerged from the darkness as his voice exploded: "Damn you! You have betrayed me! If you don't get out of here, I will shoot you! Get out of this barn at once!" The assassin reached behind his back for one of his revolvers. A terrified John Garrett turned and ran, escaping the barn.

Finally, at the climax of a twelve-day manhunt that had gripped the nation, a heavily armed patrol of the Sixteenth New York Cavalry had cornered Lincoln's assassin!

Surprisingly, instead of ordering their men to rush the barn and take Booth, they first sent an unarmed civilian to disarm him. When that scheme failed, they attempted to talk him out of the barn! Why didn't twenty-six armed soldiers, under cloak of darkness, charge two civilians hiding in a barn? Surely, the honor of capturing Lincoln's assassin was worth the risk of a few casualties?

Baker shouted an ultimatum to the fugitives: "I want you to surrender. If you don't, I will burn this barn down in fifteen minutes."

Booth stepped to the front of the barn and peered through a space between two boards, examining the man-hunters. "Who are you?" "What do you want?" "Whom do you want?"

"We want you," Baker replied, "and we know who you are. Give up your arms and come out!"

Booth continued to stall, asking for time to make a decision. Baker agreed to the delay. Herold decided to give himself up. He thought he could talk his way out of trouble and just go home. In his mind, he wasn't guilty of anything: Booth had shot Lincoln, Powell had stabbed Seward, and he had just been along for the ride.

Booth, however, refused to let Herold go. Herold pleaded with Booth, begging to be released. Finally, Booth relented, denouncing his companion: "You damned coward! . . . Go! Go!" Herold had stood by Booth, even when he had a chance to leave. He had rendered loyal service, and it was harsh to call him a coward now. Herold turned away from Booth and faced the door. He thrust one empty hand at a time through the door frame where the soldiers could see them.

Doherty sprung to the door, seized Herold by the wrists, and yanked him through the doorway. He frisked him to make sure he was unarmed and, like a schoolmaster taking a disobedient student by the collar, marched him away from the barn.

Now there remained only John Wilkes Booth, still at bay, and armed. For Booth, this was his final and greatest performance, not just for the small audience of soldiers at Garrett's barn, but also for history.

William H. Seward later in
life, showing the scar from
Lewis Powell's knife.

The surrender of David Herold at the Garrett farm

He had already committed the most daring public murder in American history. Indeed, he had *performed* it, fully staged before an audience at Ford's Theatre. Tonight he would script his own end with a performance that equaled his triumph at Ford's.

Baker and Conger argued against waiting until morning to take Booth. In a few hours, the light of dawn would illuminate the manhunters and make them into perfect, visible targets. Booth could hardly miss. One of Doherty's sergeants, Boston Corbett, volunteered for a suicide mission: He would slip into the barn alone and fight Booth one-on-one. Three times Corbett volunteered, each time Doherty ordered Corbett back to his position.

Conger and Baker had another plan: They wanted to burn the barn. The flames and smoke would do the job of flushing Booth out, without harm to the men. Conger ordered the Garrett sons to collect a few armfuls of straw and pile them against the side of the barn. The rustling sounds alerted Booth, who rushed to the site of the noise. He ordered the Garretts to move away from the barn or he would shoot them. They quickly retreated out of pistol range.

Anticipating the barn was about to be burned down, Booth challenged all of his pursuers to honorable combat on open ground. He had just challenged twenty-six men, a lieutenant, and two detectives to a duel. Baker declined the offer.

"Well, my brave boys, prepare a stretcher for me!" Booth replied merrily.

Conger bent over and lit the kindling. The pine twigs and straw burst into flames that licked the dry, weathered boards. Soon the barn caught fire, and within minutes the corner of the barn blazed brightly. The fire cast a yellow-orange glow that flickered eerily across the faces of the soldiers. Booth could see them clearly now but held his fire.

As the fire grew, it lit the inside of the barn so that for the first time the soldiers could also see their quarry in the gaps between the slats. The assassin had three choices: stay in the barn and burn alive, blow his brains out, or script his own honorable end by hobbling out the front door and doing battle with the manhunters, welcoming death but risking capture.

Booth decided it was better to die than be taken back to Washington to face justice. He did not wish to bear the spectacle of a trial that would put him on public display for the amusement of the press and curiosity seekers. Nor did he wish to endure the rituals of a hanging: being bound and blindfolded, parading past his own coffin and open grave, climbing the steps of the scaffold. The shameful death of a common criminal was not for him. It was far better to perish here.

Booth stood in the center of the barn, awkwardly balancing the carbine in one hand, a pistol in the other, and a

Printmakers hurried to publish images depicting the historic showdown at Garrett's farm.

crutch under one arm. Measuring how quickly the flames were engulfing him, he hopped forward, the carbine in his right hand, the butt plate balanced against his hip.

Outside the barn, Conger, Baker, Doherty, and the cavalrymen tensed for action. No one could endure the hot flames and choking smoke for long. They expected the door to swing open at any moment and see Booth emerge with his hands up or his pistols blazing.

Boston Corbett watched the assassin's every move inside the barn. Unseen by Booth, he walked up to one side of the barn and peeked between one of the gaps in the barn walls. As the flames grew brighter, Corbett could see his prey clearly. The sergeant watched Booth and drew his pistol. Booth leveled the carbine against his hip, as though preparing to bring it into firing position. Corbett poked the barrel of his revolver through the slit in the wall, aimed at Booth, and fired.

The soldiers heard one shot. Instantly, Booth dropped the carbine and crumpled to his knees.

Like sprinters cued by a starting gun, Baker rushed into the barn with Conger at his heels. Conger seized the assassin's pistol. They lifted Booth from the floor, carried him under the trees a few yards from the door, and laid him on the grass. Though unable to move, Booth opened his eyes and attempted to speak. Conger called for water, poured a little into Booth's mouth, and he spit it out. The assassin could not swallow, he was completely paralyzed. For the

An artist's depiction of Booth at the moment the fatal shot was fired

first time in his life, the great actor was at a loss for words. His voice was silenced by the bullet that had quickly passed through his neck and spinal column. After several attempts at speaking, Booth whispered: "Tell Mother, I die for my country." It was hard to hear his faint voice above the roar of the fire, the shouts of the men, and the snorting of the horses.

As the blaze in the barn grew to an inferno, the soldiers retreated to the Garrett house, moving Booth's limp body onto the porch near the bench where Booth had sat, smoked, napped, and chatted over the previous two days. Blood seeped from the entry and exit wounds in his neck and pooled under his head, staining the floorboards.

Doherty brought David Herold to the porch, bound his hands, and tied him to a tree about two yards from where Booth lay. Herold would have a front-row seat for the climax of the chase for Lincoln's killer.

Booth suffered extreme pain whenever he was moved. "Kill me," he begged the soldiers. "Kill me, kill me!"

"We don't want to kill you," Conger reassured him, "we want you to get well." He was sincere. They wanted Booth alive so they could bring him back to Washington as a prize for Edwin Stanton. Stanton and others were certain Booth was merely an agent of a Confederate conspiracy. Following the swearing-in of Andrew Johnson as the seventeenth president, Stanton had issued a reward for Jefferson Davis and other Confederate officials, naming them as assassination conspirators. Two other captured conspirators, Michael O'Laughlen and Sam Arnold, had already confessed everything they knew about the plot. If Booth talked, too, he might reveal valuable information that implicated the highest officials in the Confederacy.

But because of someone under Conger's command, it was obvious Booth was not going back to Washington alive. Who fired that shot? Conger demanded to know. Boston Corbett came forward, snapped to attention, saluted Conger, and proclaimed that he had shot Booth, and Providence had directed him to do it. He claimed he opened fire because he thought Booth was going to shoot the soldiers. He did it to protect the lives of his fellow troopers.

In fact, the men of the Sixteenth New York had not been ordered to hold their fire. Conger, Baker, and Doherty had failed to give them any orders at all on the subject. As a noncommissioned officer, Corbett exercised his own discretion and shot Booth.

A local doctor was summoned. He examined Booth, who lapsed in and out of consciousness. He proclaimed the wound was mortal. Booth would not recover.

Conger rifled through Booth's pockets, then placed the contents in a handkerchief. Booth's diary, money, keys, compass, small knife, and tobacco would be taken to Stanton as treasure and evidence.

"My hands," Booth whispered. Baker raised them for Booth to see. For the last time, John Wilkes Booth saw the hands, now helpless, that had slain Abraham Lincoln. Gathering his remaining strength, he looked at his hands and spoke his last words: "Useless, useless." Booth's lips turned purple and his throat swelled. He gasped.

The rising sun nudged above the horizon and colored the eastern sky, flooding the Garrett farm with light, which shone on Booth's face. The stage grew dark for him. His body shuddered. John Wilkes Booth was dead. The twelve-day chase for Abraham Lincoln's assassin was over.

Sergt. BOSTON CORBETT, 16th N. Y. Cav.,
Who shot J. WILKES BOOTH, April 26, 1865.

Entered according to Act of Congress, by M. B. Brady & Co., in the year 1865
n the Clerk's Office of the District Court for the District of Columbia.

Brady   *Washington.*

THE LIFE, CRIME, AND CAPTURE

OF

John Wilkes Booth

AND THE PURSUIT, TRIAL AND EXECUTION OF HIS ACCOMPLICES.

NEW YORK:

DICK & FITZGERALD, PUBLISHERS.

Copies of this work mailed to any address free of Postage.

Booth dominated the cover of an important book about the assassination and trial

CHAPTER XII

Lieutenant Doherty unrolled his wool army blanket and ordered his men to lay Booth's body upon it. With needle and thread provided by the Garretts, he sewed the blanket closed around the assassin's corpse. Soldiers heaved the corpse like a sack of corn onto the wagon that would bring the body to its first stop on the journey back to Washington. The body was transferred from the wagon to a rowboat, then to a steamboat, which would then take them north to Washington.

Conger rode ahead of the body, rushing to be the first of the manhunters to tell Stanton that Booth had been found and killed. He also hoped to precede the rest of the cavalry and stake the first claim to the reward money. Conger and Baker laid out Booth's possessions on a table. Stanton picked up the diary, then the compass. The hunt was over.

To be absolutely certain the body was Booth's, Stanton ordered an inquest and autopsy. A few people were allowed to see the corpse for purposes of identification. The cause of death was easily determined: gunshot via a single bullet through the neck. Stanton had Booth's corpse photographed.

News of Booth's death traveled across the nation by telegraph, and newspapers rushed to print stories filled with the details of the manhunt's climax at Garrett's farm. Reporters seeking a great story sought to uncover the final act of Booth's life: the disposal of the assassin's remains. Luther Baker refused to reveal the body's location. After staging a false "burial at sea" to throw the press off the trail, Booth's body was buried in a simple crate in an unmarked grave at the Old Arsenal Penitentiary. His fellow conspirators would soon join him there.

Chapter XIII

Thomas Jones, Captain Cox, the Garrett sons, and many more were seized and taken to prison. Curiously, within weeks, Stanton freed them all. He put on trial only eight defendants: Mary Surratt, Lewis Powell, David Herold, George Atzerodt, Samuel Arnold, Michael O'Laughlen, Edman Spangler, and Samuel Mudd. Not one person who helped Booth and Herold during their escape, except Dr. Mudd, was punished. They returned to their homes and families and, for years to come, whispered secret tales of their deeds during the great manhunt.

Another hunt, the one for reward money, began before Booth's corpse had even cooled. With Booth dead, and his chief accomplices under arrest, awaiting trial, it was time to cash in. Hundreds of manhunters rushed to claim a portion of the $100,000 reward offered by the War Department. Tipsters with the slightest connection to the twelve-day search for Lincoln's killer tried to get their piece of the reward. More than a year after the manhunt ended, the government

Six of the alleged conspirators were first confined aboard the ironclad ships *Montauk* and *Saugus* on April 27, 1865. One by one, they were brought up to the deck, seated before the gun turret, and presented to the photographer.

David Herold. Sentenced to death by hanging.

George Atzerodt. Sentenced to death by hanging.

Samuel Arnold. Conspirator in Booth's original plot to kidnap President Lincoln. Sentenced to life in prison.

Michael O'Laughlen. Conspirator in the kidnapping plot. Sentenced to life in prison.

Edman Spangler. Found guilty and sentenced to prison, he was actually innocent of all charges.

A pamphlet about the assassination and the trial of the conspirators

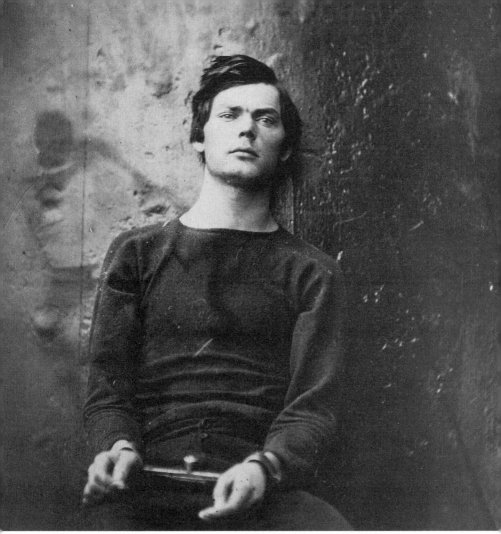

Powell sits against the battle-scarred turret of the ironclad *Montauk*, where he and other male conspirators were held prior to their confinement in the Old Arsenal Prison. Powell's wrist irons are clearly visible.

Haunting images of Powell, photographed on board the Montauk. More photographs were taken of him than any of the other conspirators.

finally paid out the rewards. Congress paid Conger $15,000, Doherty $5,250, Lafayette Baker $3,750, Luther Baker $3,000. Boston Corbett, along with every noncommissioned officer at the barn, received $1,653. Colonel Wells and other interrogators received $500 to $1,000 each for their roles in the hunt. Nine men received smaller rewards for their part in the capture of George Atzerodt, ten for their roles in the arrest of Lewis Powell.

Richard Garrett made a claim against the U.S. government for compensation, for the value of his property, including the burned barn and the corn and hay consumed by the cavalry horses. The government considered his claim but refused to pay him a cent. After all, he had been disloyal to the Union.

Boston Corbett was never punished for shooting Booth. He had violated no orders, and no one could prove his motive was anything other than protecting his men. He enjoyed both fame and notoriety for a brief time. Then he went mad and disappeared.

CHAPTER XIV
TRIAL
&EXECUTION

On the morning of July 6, 1865, the clock began ticking on one of the most dramatic events in the history of Washington, the climactic event of the manhunt. It had been two and a half months since the death of John Wilkes Booth. An officer left the War Department and delivered death warrants to the defendants Mary Surratt, David Herold, George Atzerodt, and Lewis Powell. They would be hanged tomorrow morning. The rapid conviction, sentencing, and execution of the Lincoln assassination conspirators concluded the trial that had lasted through May and June. Four of Booth's helpers and henchmen, Edman Spangler, Michael O'Laughlen, Samuel Arnold, and Dr. Samuel Mudd, received prison sentences.

Booth was already dead, so four of the eight conspirators who had been put on trial took center stage on execution day. The soldiers in the Old Arsenal Penitentiary hurriedly

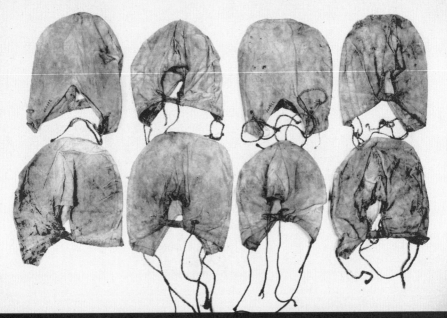

Canvas hoods were worn by most of the conspirators during much of their stay in prison.

A depiction of Lewis Powell in his cell at the Old Arsenal Prison during his trial, hooded and restrained by wrist irons

constructed a scaffold, dug graves, and prepared coffins for the four convicts. On July 7, the prisoners were paraded onto the scaffold. The condemned were bound and hooded. Nooses were slipped over their necks and, at 1:26 P.M., they dropped to their deaths. Lewis Powell, David Herold, and George Atzerodt reunited in the grave with John Wilkes Booth, together again, as they had been that terrible evening of April 1865, when the chase for Lincoln's killer began.

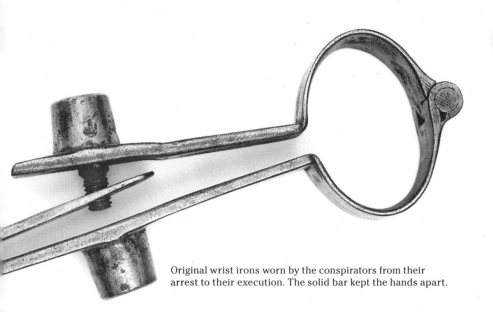

Original wrist irons worn by the conspirators from their arrest to their execution. The solid bar kept the hands apart.

From left to right: Mary Surratt, Lewis Powell, David Herold, and George Atzerodt, hanging in death

July 7, 1865. The condemned are prepared for execution.

This engraving, from a book containing the transcript of the conspirators' trial, reflects the government's claim that Mary Surratt was at the center of the conspiracy.

EPILOGUE

In 1869, President Andrew Johnson released the body of John Wilkes Booth to the assassin's brother, Edwin, who had him buried quietly in the family plot at Green Mount Cemetery in Baltimore, Maryland. He lies there still, but no headstone marks his grave.

Edwin Stanton continued to serve as secretary of war during the difficult times of Andrew Johnson's presidency. Johnson tried to fire him, but Stanton refused to surrender his War Department offices. General Ulysses Grant became President Grant in 1869, and nominated Stanton to the Supreme Court. Sadly, Stanton died before he could join the court.

Secretary of State William H. Seward and his sons survived their wounds. For the rest of his life until his death in 1872, he preferred to turn the scarred half of his face away from the camera. Sadly, two months after the Lincoln assassination, Seward's wife died. The following year, his daughter, Fanny, died from tuberculosis.

Clara Harris and Henry Rathbone married, but eighteen years later he went insane and murdered her, using a gun and knife, the same type of weapons Booth carried the night he killed Abraham Lincoln.

Thomas Jones kept the secrets of the pine thicket until, almost twenty years later, he told his tale to a writer. He later wrote his own book about his adventures with John Wilkes Booth.

Lafayette Baker also published a book about the manhunt, exaggerating his role in the chase for Booth. He died in 1868.

John Harrison Surratt was eventually tracked down through Canada to Europe, where he served, under a false name, in the pope's army. He was chased to Egypt, captured, and in 1867 brought back to America for trial. In 1868, after a trial failed to reach a verdict and charges were dismissed, he was released, a free man. But he earned the reputation of a coward who had abandoned his mother to die.

Dr. Samuel A. Mudd was imprisoned in Florida, but his sentence was commuted by President Johnson, partly for assistance during an outbreak of illness in the prison. He returned to his farm in 1869. Before he died in 1883, he confessed to Samuel Cox Jr. that he had known all along that the injured stranger at his door was John Wilkes Booth.

Ford's Theatre, restored in the 1960s after serving as a

government office building, lives again as a museum and working playhouse. Presidents come here again to attend plays, but out of respect for Abraham Lincoln, none sits in the president's box. The restoration of the theater was meant as a tribute to Abraham Lincoln, but Ford's has also become a memorial to his assassin.

If Booth could return today to the scene of his crime and visit, as one million visitors do every year, the basement museum at Ford's, he might conclude, from what he found there, that it was again April 14, 1865. He would find preserved, in climate-controlled, shatterproof display cases, the prized relics of the assassination: the original door to the president's box, its peephole still luring curious eyes; his revolvers and knives; the carbine Booth and Herold picked up on their midnight run to Surratt's tavern; his whistle and keys; photos of his sweethearts, his pocket diary, its pages still open, as if awaiting another entry; his Deringer pistol; and, resting in its velvet-lined box, his pocket compass, which guided him during his dangerous days on the run.

John Wilkes Booth did not get what he wanted. Yes, he did kill Abraham Lincoln, but in every other way, Booth was a failure. He did not inspire the South to fight on, prolong the Civil War, or win the battles the Confederate armies had lost. He did not undo the Emancipation Proclamation and revive slavery.

And yet we still remember Booth to this day. But he is not the hero of the story. The real hero is Abraham Lincoln and the principles for which he lived — and died: freedom and equal rights for all Americans.

If Ford's Theatre is Booth's place, then across the street there is a memorial to Abraham Lincoln. But many people do not even know it exists. Few visitors to Ford's cross 10th Street and climb the stairs to the Petersen house. If you go there today, you can walk to the tiny back bedroom and stand in the same place where Lincoln's family and friends once stood around his deathbed, bidding him farewell, but vowing to continue his unfinished work.

ABOUT THE AUTHOR

★★★★★★★★★★★★★★★★★★★★★★★★★★★★★

James L. Swanson is the author of the *New York Times* bestseller *Manhunt: The 12-Day Chase for Lincoln's Killer,* upon which this book is based. *Manhunt* received an Edgar Award for the best true crime book of the year in 2007. His other books include the photographic history *Lincoln's Assassins: Their Trial and Execution.* He serves on the advisory council of the Ford's Theatre Society, and is a member of the advisory committee of the national Abraham Lincoln Bicentennial Commission. He is a lawyer in Washington, D.C., where he has held a number of government and think-tank posts. Born on Lincoln's birthday, he has collected books, documents, and artifacts about the life and death of Abraham Lincoln since he was ten years old. This is his first young adult book.

ACKNOWLE

My wife, Andrea E. Mays, an astute critic, reader, and writer of historical nonfiction, read and commented on the manuscript from her unique perspective. She read several drafts, saved me from making a number of embarrassing errors and omissions, and improved the book in countless ways. Without her help, *Chasing Lincoln's Killer* would not exist.

I thank my two chief young readers and advisors, Cameron and Harrison, who asked unexpected questions during their first visit to Ford's Theatre and who, at the ages of eleven and nine, have already exhibited remarkable storytelling flair. I look forward to reading their books someday. Cameron read *Manhunt: The 12-Day Chase for Lincoln's Killer*, the adult version of this book, and also listened to it on audio before making helpful observations and comments. Harrison helped in choosing just the right words, remarking, for example, that "henchman" would speak to children in a way that "co-conspirator" would not. Thanks also to my niece Samantha for inviting me to speak to her second-grade writing class, where the students prepared a list of tips on how to write for young adults, including this classic: "Keep in all the blood and gore, but not so much that our parents flip out." My younger niece Nicky echoed this bloodthirsty taste.

Thanks to my friends at the Library of Congress, the National Archives, the William H. Seward House, the Surratt Society, and at many other libraries and museums who helped me write this book. I wish that I could name them all.

CKNOWLEDGMENTS

Richard Abate, my literary agent, offered his enthusiasm, insights, and friendship. He made this a better book.

I thank all my friends at Scholastic for their hard work in publishing this book. I owe special thanks to my editor, Andrea Davis Pinkney, who introduced me to the world of writing for young adults, and who guided me with a steady hand every step along the way.

My own hunt for John Wilkes Booth began when my grandmother, Elizabeth, a veteran of Chicago's legendary and now extinct tabloid newspaper scene, gave a ten-year-old boy the unusual gift of a framed engraving of Booth's Deringer pistol, along with an April 15, 1865, *Chicago Tribune* clipping, thus triggering the fascination that led to this book. This is in memory of her.

My sister Denise's animated spirit and taste for strange historical tales encouraged me from the start. From an early age, she aided and abetted my literary pursuits.

Finally, I thank my parents, Dianne and Lennart Swanson. Without their love and generous support over many years, I never could have written *Chasing Lincoln's Killer*, or anything else.

★★ **JAMES L.** ★★
SWANSON
WASHINGTON, D.C. AUGUST 1, 2008

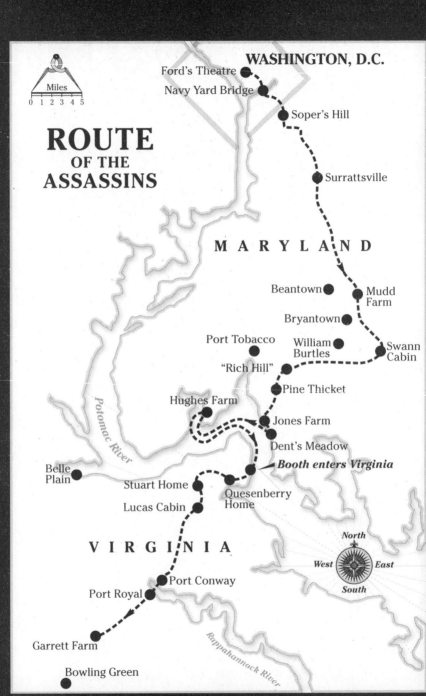

ROUTE
OF THE
ASSASSINS

Miles
0 1 2 3 4 5

WASHINGTON, D.C.

Ford's Theatre

Navy Yard Bridge

Soper's Hill

Surrattsville

M A R Y L A N D

Beantown

Mudd Farm

Bryantown

Port Tobacco

William Burtles

Swann Cabin

"Rich Hill"

Pine Thicket

Hughes Farm

Jones Farm

Dent's Meadow

Booth enters Virginia

Belle Plain

Potomac River

Stuart Home

Lucas Cabin

Quesenberry Home

V I R G I N I A

North

West   East

South

Port Conway

Port Royal

Garrett Farm

Bowling Green

Rappahannock River